A Hand
On My
Shoulder

A Hand
On My
Shoulder

*God's Miraculous Touch
On My Life*

Myrtle Dorthea Monville Beall

Edited by
K. Joy Hughes Gruits

Copyright © 2017 K. Joy Hughes Gruits

All rights reserved. This book or any portion thereof may not be reproduced or used in any manner whatsoever without the express written permission of the publisher except for the use of brief quotations in a book review or scholarly journal.

Unless otherwise indicated, Scripture quotations in this book are taken from The Holy Bible, the KING JAMES VERSION (KJV): KING JAMES VERSION, public domain.

Scriptures marked NKJV are taken from the NEW KING JAMES VERSION (NKJV): Scripture taken from the NEW KING JAMES VERSION®. Copyright© 1982 by Thomas Nelson, Inc. Used by permission. All rights reserved.

Scriptures marked AMP are taken from the AMPLIFIED BIBLE (AMP): Scripture taken from the AMPLIFIED® BIBLE, Copyright © 1954, 1958, 1962, 1964, 1965, 1987 by the Lockman Foundation Used by Permission.

Cover design by Jeana Nowaczewski

First Printing: 2014 (1)
Second Printing: 2017

ISBN: 5 8000106 993672
ISBN: 13.978-1976218224

Web Address: www.embracehiscall.com

Publisher:
K. Joy Hughes Gruits
1359 New Love Lane
Rochester Hills, Michigan 48309

To Patricia Beall Gruits

A daughter who faithfully continued the
spiritual legacy of her mother

FOREWORD

Myrtle Dorthea Monville Beall was affectionately known as "Mom Beall" to many and respectfully addressed as Pastor M.D. Beall by others. I was blessed to know her as Grandma Beall, not because I was her granddaughter but because I married her grandson, Joe. I remember pot roast meals with corn on the cob, no matter the season, and always way too much food for the three of us to eat. At Christmas time, Joe would string her lights and then we would join her in the study, her favorite room, knowing this was the place where many bold prayers had been prayed. This was the place where God gave her the succinct and powerful messages she would preach each Sunday—messages that would lead us to the altar to be touched by God's presence again and again. When Grandma preached, it was not a canned message, it wasn't a theological dissertation, it was a fresh and living Word that strengthened your faith and challenged your walk with the Lord.

What made her unique among the great preachers of her day was that she had a uniquely intimate relationship with the Lord. He put His Hand on her shoulder from a young age and revealed Himself more fully as the years passed. She was known as one who truly knew the Voice of God and was obedient, no matter the cost. Hers was an extraordinary life of faith, a life that left an eternal imprint on countless lives of others.

In the 1950's Grandma Beall was encouraged to document her journey of faith. Jo Burbank, who became acquainted with Grandma Beall through the radio program "America To Her Knees," wrote as Grandma dictated the story of her life and ministry. A manuscript was started in 1952 and subsequent chapters were drafted until the year 1956. Although chapters of her journey were printed in the church's monthly publication called "Latter Rain Evangel," the chapters of this memoir had never been published together as a complete story and had laid dormant for over 60 years. At the request of Patricia Beall Gruits, her daughter, I have edited the manuscript. The goal of the edits was to tell her story in chronological order, clarifying her spiritual journey, filling in the gaps when possible and eliminating the repetitions, but in the process still retaining "her voice."

In Moses' final address to the Israelites before they crossed into the Promised Land, he exhorted them: "Remember how the LORD your God led you all the way in the wilderness." *(Deut. 8:2)* It was important to God that the Israelites from generation to generation would always remember what God had done for them. This book, *A Hand on My Shoulder*, was written so that we would not forget what God had done through this woman named Myrtle Beall. That her journey from a young girl in a small mining town in Michigan's Upper Peninsula to an influential pastor whom God used to build an "Armory," where thousands of people were spiritually equipped to fulfill their divine purpose, would not be forgotten. As you follow her journey, as you learn what God did for her, may the Lord put His Hand on your shoulder and lead you, as He did Grandma, to a deeper relationship with Him.

K. Joy Hughes Gruits
September 2017

Pastor M.D. Beall

Chapter 1

The First Touch

When I was a child, suddenly in the midst of a child's duties or pleasures, I would often feel the touch of a *hand on my shoulder*—a gentle touch but yet a firm one; the touch of a loving hand but a hand that bespoke authority. Always I would turn to see who had touched me so, but I never found anyone there. The experience, frequently repeated, left me with a strange feeling of questioning. But I never told anyone of the hand on my shoulder or asked a grown-up to explain it to me, for it was a very private experience. Many a childhood hour was spent in wondering what it meant. Many a year was to pass before I found the answer.

There was nothing in my background, circumstances, or family that would account for such a strange, almost supernatural, occurrence. On the contrary, mine was a most normal childhood and way of life, unless great happiness and love would be considered abnormal. This love and happiness were spread about me like a warm mantle by the hands of my parents, and around my three brothers and two sisters as well.

This capacity for love and their large, happy family were my parents' only real distinction. My father, Joseph Monville, was born in Port Huron, Michigan of French and Scottish parentage. At the time of my birth on December 9, 1894, he worked in a copper mill in the Upper Peninsula (U.P.) of Michigan, in the little town of Hubbell in the heart of the Copper Country, where we made our home.

A Hand On My Shoulder

My mother, Mary Margaret Harrington, was born in county Cork, Ireland and came to American in her teens. Like my father, she was a devout Catholic. A few days after I was born, as was the Catholic custom, I was taken to the church to be christened. My mother had chosen an honest and classic Irish name—Brigadine or Bridget, for short. From the heavy responsibility of bearing such a cognomen, I was at the last moment rescued by my aunt, who was acting as my godmother. She elected that I be called Myrtle, and I have been everlastingly grateful for her forethought.

As Myrtle Monville, then, I began my happy childhood. Though my parents' means were modest, by some magic we always had a sound home, plenty to eat, and nice clothing. The needs of the body neither overshadowed nor precluded the needs for the mind and soul, for my parents were also intent upon our having an education as well - an aim not too common among parents of comparable resources in those days.

Consequently, at the age of seven I entered St. Cecilia's Convent School under the splendid training of the nuns and the oversight of Rev. Father H. Zimmerman, a very godly priest. I have never ceased thanking God for my early training under these godly people, where I remained until I was 13 years of age. This was followed by attendance at the Lake Linden High School in Lake Linden, Michigan, and eventually by matriculation at Michigan State Normal College in Ypsilanti, where I was to train for teaching.

My school days were happy and exciting ones. With my brothers and sisters I played freely without fear, enjoying the wonderful sports, the great U.P. outdoors with its stimulating climate and broad, shimmering lakes. I also thoroughly enjoyed school, not merely in its academic phases, but also in the matchless opportunity to know and share life with my schoolmates. I was proud to be a member of my high school basketball team for a full four years—a team which won the championship for the entire state!

We especially enjoyed the wonderful northern Christmas season, when we would go to the hills to fell one of the pine trees which grew so profusely there. Though we could never afford the expensive, flittering decorations some enjoyed, we were perfectly content stringing cranberries and popcorn, making popcorn balls, and hanging them with apples and oranges on the tree. Most important of all the decorations, my mother used to hang a large candy cane for each of us on the lower branches of the tree. We used to slip under and take bites off the sticks until little was left but the handle. I had a cousin, an only child who lived near us, whose Christmas tree fairly shimmered with costly tinsel and ornaments, but he didn't like it. He preferred to visit our tree and take bites off his candy cane from underneath the boughs!

Yes, I always loved fun, and I had my full share of it. My brothers, sisters and I, like most normal children, played and laughed and capered, sometimes to the point of boisterousness. There must have been many times when we were trying in our exuberance, but I never remember at any time my father raising a hand to any of us in chastisement. The worst I can remember was the time when my father was entertaining company. I disturbed him to the point at which he said to me quietly, "I've got my eye on you!" It is scarcely necessary to say that was as far as I went. I was crushed to think that I had hurt him—the best father in the world and the essence of kindness always.

Some of this kindness and thoughtfulness was no doubt inherited. My father's mother was a lovely and lovable person. She was called the "mother" of the village in which she lived. When she died at the end of a long and useful life, even the school bells tolled as her funeral procession wound slowly down the village street. Whenever my father or any of his brothers spoke of their mother, they did so in awed tones and with raised hats. From what I have gathered from those who knew her, she was a born-again Christian.

It was from his mother that my father drew the love, goodness, and tolerant understanding that marked him through life and was reflected upon my mother and us children. A hard-working man, he never failed to come home and give his full pay envelope, unopened, to my mother, who surely had enough to do with it. A good manager and a good wife, she nevertheless had her hands full and her purse near emptiness with six children to feed and clothe. I never had the privilege of knowing my mother's parents, who remained in Ireland when she immigrated to America, though by all reports they were good and God-fearing people.

Later in life my maternal aunt died, and my mother raised her oldest son—a baby just a few months old, Joseph Harrington. But in our home and in my parents' large hearts, there was always room for one more. We never knew by precept or example what it meant to deny anyone a portion of what little we had. The guiding principles of my parents' lives were generosity and to help others in unremitting measure.

One incident is typical. After my mother died, we had a Holland hot air furnace installed in our home. One year when my siblings and I went Up North to visit Dad, we found the furnace missing. When we asked him what happened to it, he replied that he had given it to the widow down the street who had babies creeping on a cold floor. He said, "I can get along without it."

From this and many other occurrences which I could relate, it was evident that his Christianity was not confined to kneeling and praying, which was a common thing for us to see him do any time of the day or evening, upon arising or retiring. But surely his was a way of life that spoke much more loudly than oral professions.

Indeed, religion as a profession was not a feature of any of our lives, much less an expectation that a call to preach the Gospel of Jesus Christ should be given to one of us. Yet, that call came to me years later at a time when I was myself the mother of three small children.

In recent years, the urging of my friends and fellows all over the country to tell the strange story of how this came about has grown until I can no longer plead lack of literary ability. And because God moves in miraculous ways to prove His faithfulness in enabling those

He calls, I have at last been led to put down on paper the events that led to and followed my surrender to His plan of life.

What I write here, with sincerity if not with the inspiration of genius, is only what I have myself experienced, learned, and felt in these more than thirty years. It is written in wonderment that these incidents should be of interest to others, and I write it only in the hope that it may be a small tool of God for the accomplishment of good. Like Paul at Ephesus, I am in the deep debt of others, so many others that I find it impossible to list their names in these pages. Suffice it to say that those who have touched my life, for good or ill, constitute a great multitude.

And the first touch was the touch of an unseen hand on my shoulder as a child—a *Hand* that was not there when I turned, a *Hand* that shall guide mine as I write the pages to come.

Chapter 2

Learning Many Lessons

One of the strange paradoxes in life is to feel a part of something and yet apart from that very something—a sense of abstraction in the middle of a social gathering; a sudden remoteness in the midst of active participation in a group activity; an inexplicable and involuntary withdrawal, for perhaps only a moment, from a situation with which one is closely identified. For most, this feeling is one which comes rarely. But in my case, it was an ever-present knowledge which continued throughout my childhood years. My family was a loving, close-knit one, and I was, and felt I was, a very close part of it. Yet in many ways I always felt like the "odd sheep," and in a manner I cannot describe. I always felt apart from them—somehow different, somehow singled out.

I have a most vivid memory of an event that occurred when I was a young girl, perhaps ten or eleven years of age. On a summer evening, I was outdoors playing with my older sister and other children, playing around the street light in front of our home, a favorite area for our pastimes. We were having an even livelier time than usual. The laughter was louder, the fun more strenuous, when suddenly I felt the now- familiar touch of the Hand upon my shoulder.

A sudden feeling of the need to call upon God swept over me like an irresistible wave. Scarcely knowing what I was doing, I began to repeat the Lord's Prayer over and over again: "Our Father which art in Heaven . . . Our Father which art in Heaven . . ."

As the sensation increased in intensity, moment after moment, I became weaker even to the point of perspiring in the anxiety and the pressure of the intolerable burden. In a small, pleading voice, I begged my older sister, Mary, to stop playing and come with me to the porch where I had something to confide in her. She was absorbed in her pleasure, but at last I prevailed upon her to leave the group and accompany me to the porch, where we both sat on my dad's old wicker rocker.

Provoked at stopping her play, she asked me again and again what was the matter with me. Why did I break up the fun? I replied falteringly that I felt very troubled, for I feared something was happening to someone who needed my prayers, and I felt constrained to offer up those prayers.

My sister looked at me unbelievingly. This was not like me. Far from being a pious child, I was one that loved to play and have fun, one that indeed was usually the ringleader in the pursuit of games and laughter. At any rate, she made it clear that she did not share my sensations and declared that as I had spoiled the fun and was talking nonsense, so she might as well go to bed.

I begged her not to leave me, to stay until I learned what the trouble was, for I felt it growing ever closer at hand. But she insisted on going to bed. Rather than being left alone, I followed her there. Far from sleep, I sat upright in bed with my arms around my knees waiting—waiting for the catastrophe that was sure to come.

Suddenly I heard footsteps and voices in the street, coming nearer increasing in volume. As I sprang out of bed, I called to my sister, "There it is!"

We both ran down the stairs and out onto the porch, which was being mounted by a group of men who were carrying the still form of my brother. He had been terribly burned almost beyond recognition by an accidental explosion of some fireworks intended for the Fourth of July. In the midst of my horror, sadness, and fear, I yet thanked God that He would account me worthy to lay a burden of prayer upon me, small and weak though I was. Again I began to repeat the Lord's Prayer over and over, scarcely knowing what I was saying, but inalterably convinced that I was at least talking directly to God.

I found then, and the knowledge has been confirmed many times since, that God can lay a burden on a child, that God can even call a child to prayer, and He will answer. My brother recovered completely, without even a scar.

* * *

A Hand On My Shoulder

Happy the child, and later the grown-up, who has happy memories of his school days. I have such fond remembrances of my years in St. Cecilia's Convent School, where my life was touched and enriched by the teaching of the Sisters of the Franciscan Order, whom I learned to love, respect, and reverence. I recall clearly at the age of eleven in the seventh grade, how my classmates and I used to attend Lenten services given by our parish priest, a kindly, good-humored cleric of German extraction. It was our task after a sermon to submit an essay on what we had gleaned from his preaching. It was a never-ending source of amusement and amazement to Father Zimmerman to read my searching and ingenious interpretations of his messages, so different from the simple and conventional analyses of my classmates. I loved him, and he loved me, but that did not save me from his continual teasing about my Christian name, Myrtle, because it was not a Catholic saint's name according to the custom.

In his slight Teutonic accent he would repeat, "Who ever heard of a St. Myrtle?" Then he and all the children would laugh, much to my embarrassment. Finally one day, when I felt I could stand the taunting no longer and my "Irish rose up," I retorted sharply, "Someday when I die, there will be a Saint Myrtle!" This, of course, only served to redouble the laughter, but the good Father, needless to say, teased me no longer.

I had not yet learned then, as I know now, that God is as interested in living saints as He is in those who have died, and that His love and grace are poured out upon them in no lesser measure because they still walk on earth. But though that lesson was yet to come, I did learn many others both academic and spiritual as the touch of *His Hand* upon my shoulder lingered longer and pressed more firmly each time it rested upon me.

Chapter 3

The Busy Years Bring Change

The pleasant memories of my life at St. Cecelia's Convent School have followed me through the years. Few children, I am sure, can thank God for happier school days. Yet, as is the nature of youth, I looked forward almost breathlessly to high school and the new knowledge, the new acquaintances, the new experiences it promised.

After graduating from St. Cecilia's at the age of twelve, I entered high school in nearby Lake Linden, and there I stayed until I was 16. Here, though more ordered and organized, my intense enjoyment of play and social life continued. I was one of the school's star basketball players for a full four years, had the leading part in our senior play, loved the athletics, the school dances and parties, and other activities with which high school life is pleasantly rife. I enjoyed existence to the fullest, even the two-and-a-half mile walk to school through the deep Up North snows, which with my schoolmates was merely one more occasion for laughter and fun.

Nor was my academic life neglected. I took four years of Latin, two years of German, along with chemistry, history and the other usual college preparatory courses. I took part in many declamation and oratorical contests as well. But these years, too, came to an end as everything must, and at 16 I graduated from high school and enrolled in the Michigan State Teacher's College in Ypsilanti, Michigan.

Here, however, Fate took a hand. Before graduating from college, I was offered a tempting position in a department store in my home town of Hubbell. Impulsively, I accepted and returned home to make preparations for my entrance into the business world. It is strange how certain scenes in one's past life remain vividly in the mind's eye

A Hand On My Shoulder

without having their clarity dimmed by the passing of the years. On my way home from college, crossing the Straits of Mackinaw on the ferry, I was thrilled to find among the passengers a Militia, fine young men in uniform, bubbling over with the vigor and excitement of youth away from home grounds. They had been dispatched to keep order at the copper mines during a strike and were returning from duty. I can hear them now singing a song, the lyrics of which went:

> "In the Copper Range Mountains of the U.P.
> On guard at the mines, you see . . ."

Little did I think, as I looked and listened with admiration, that these and most of our other young men would again be in uniform for a longer time and on a graver and more dangerous mission—the First World War.

* * *

It was during the period between my return from college and my beginnings in the commercial world, that again I felt the now familiar touch of the *Hand* on my shoulder—this time in the unlikely surroundings of a community dance. When I felt the touch, an awesome sensation crept over me which I know now, but did not realize then, was the anointing power of the Almighty. I trembled and felt strangely arrested of God, and my companions, frightened, asked me if I felt ill or if I was cold. But it was neither of these. It was something different than I had ever experienced in my life up until that moment. Yet I thank God that during the years of my ministry since, I have felt the same sensation many, many times.

I do not believe that Saul of Tarsus felt more arrested on the road to Damascus than I felt that night at the dance. A thousand strange thoughts and wonders crowded my mind, but I buried all this in my heart, not knowing what it meant. As did Mary in the scriptural passage where it was said of her: ". . . and Mary pondered all these things in her heart." *(Luke 2:19)*

* * *

For five years I worked in the Toplon Department Store, assisted in the buying and enjoyed myself immensely. But all the boys and

The Busy Years Bring Change

many of the young women of Hubbell were beginning to leave our little town for the big cities, where enticing wages were being offered. The war had brought a great increase in manufacturing, and indeed in all commercial pursuits, and the need for more workers was great and compensated accordingly. Friend after friend departed the city wards. And in time, I was attracted by the call. My closest girl friend and I decided to share in the adventure and excitement, and found ourselves preparing to leave.

But like all youth, I little realized what my leaving would mean to my father and mother. I did not understand their fear and trepidation at seeing a young girl, green and unacquainted with the ways of the world, trusting everyone and believing all to be one's friend, starting unthinkingly for a big and heartless city. Mother and Dad told me later that although they did not wish to interfere with my plans for my life, it seemed like everything stopped when I left. For years afterward, whenever my Dad would hear the trains whistle, he would go to the window and murmur, half mournfully, half resentfully: 'There goes the Robber!"

However, in the excitement and anticipation of our leaving, I gave little thought to all this. When we went to the depot, practically the whole town turned out to see us off, as we had lived, played, and worked right there all of our lives and were dear to them all. My dad, despite his disappointment, came to see us off and with him was my mother's little nephew, Joseph, about five years old, whom we had raised from infancy. When the time actually came to board the train, I felt I just couldn't stand to go, leaving the dear little fellow and my loving parents. Of course, my girlfriend was going through the same contradictory agony. But finally the train pulled out slowly, taking us away from all we knew and loved. The gifts, candy, and fruit with which our friends had laden us was poor compensation for the tears that streamed down our cheeks.

After we found our seats, we could not even talk to each other. We were going hundreds of miles away, and the strange and wonderful names of Milwaukee, Chicago, and Cleveland seemed to belong to another and forbidding planet. We sat and sobbed until it was time for us to go to bed. Of course, neither of us had ever been in a train berth in our lives, and the problem of what to do with our fruit and candy was a puzzler. Finally we decided to put them on a little ledge behind us. We managed to put out the light, and then could not find how to turn it on again. The ridiculousness of the situation turned our tears to giggles, as the plums, oranges, and apples began to drop down on our heads. What we had thought to be a ledge turned out not to be!

There we were, unable to turn on the light, fruit dropping on our heads, bananas and candy squashed under our wriggling bodies, and the sounds of our mirth increasing until at last the porter, summoned no doubt by outraged passengers, came and turned on our light and threatened to put us off the train. But when he saw our predicament, he stifled a giggle of his own and helped to clean up the mess. At last we quieted down, much to our own relief and, I am sure, that of the other occupants of the train.

And so I was on my way. Here the destiny of my life turned. I was on my way to the city where I was to meet my husband. On my way to the fulfillment of God's secret plan for me with not a hint of what He had planned to bring to pass in my life, with not a dream of what lay before me.

Chapter 4

God Plans My Training For The Future

In my early twenties, having made a success of my business life in my home town, I experienced the urge to enter a larger arena of action. I felt I had something to sell that the world wanted, and in a city the size of Cleveland my opportunities would be greatly expanded. Accordingly, I made the journey to the "pulse of the Middle West."

I was in Cleveland only one month when I was offered a position to assist the buyer of ladies' wear in its largest department store. But God, who was ordering my life, decreed otherwise. I had neither relatives nor friends in Cleveland, and I was persuaded by a loved one to go to the city of Detroit, where I could be near my brother, Jack, my only relative in that city.

Although I did not realize it, it was in Detroit that God would begin my training for the ministry—that difficult combination of spiritual, humane, and practical activities so vitally necessary for doing His work upon earth among men. I began work in the welfare department of a large business concern, the Champion Sparkplug Company, and also helped in first-aid work. God blessed my efforts and soon I was invited to work in the pay office and take charge of the payroll. Thus, step by step, Providence led me along the path to His work: training in meeting the public, in filling the spiritual and corporal needs of people in welfare and first-aid work, and finally in the administration of finances. As I look back, I can see the heavenly blueprint in action, and I thank God for this invaluable preparation for His work.

It was while working in the pay office that I met Harry Lee Beall. Happy and fun-loving as I had always been, I had many male admirers and was, in fact, even at the point of accepting an engagement ring. But when it came to actually marrying, I was not truly interested until I met Harry Beall.

One day a little Southern girl in my office remarked with enthusiasm: "Say, have you met Mr. Beall? He has just returned from the service and is he nice!" With some amusement at her remark, I replied that I had not met the gentleman. Nothing would do for her except to bring Mr. Beall to the pay office window right then and there to meet me. After I saw and spoke to him, I was constrained to say to myself, "Well, he is nice."

Harry was a department foreman, and it was surprising how frequently he found it necessary to call at the pay office window to discuss imaginary payroll discrepancies connected with his department. Strangely, amid the banter and conversational exploration of each other's tastes and backgrounds, so eternally characteristic of a young man and woman in such a situation, I could not help but sense that our lives had crossed paths to a more serious purpose. And it seemed that he knew it, too. I am convinced that we cared for each other from the very start.

But an age-old and seemingly insurmountable barrier was interposed between us. We were of different faiths, and each confirmed in the belief that ours was the right way. I had been raised in Catholicism, and Harry was a Protestant and a Mason. Neither of us could imagine for a moment the possibility of adopting the other's faith in marriage. We both suffered much, not knowing what to do. One moment we would decide we must stop seeing each other, the next we knew we could not bear the idea of separation.

* * *

One Sunday we were invited for dinner at the home of friends and co-workers. While we were sitting in the living room waiting for dinner to be served, I idly picked up a little black book, being an inveterate lover of reading. Upon opening it at random, I discovered it was a small Bible.

I was, like most Catholics, not intimately acquainted with Bibles. Catholics are not encouraged to read and literally interpret the Bible, so my knowledge of Scripture had only been gleaned through a Bible history class and official ecclesiastical interpretations of the Holy

God Plans My Training for the Future

Book. Actually, at this time I had never before had a Bible in my hand, so naturally I was not prepared for its contents. Having opened it at random, I found that the page was one in the book of Ruth. The heading at the top of the page held no significance for me, but I have realized since that God must have guided my idle fingers as I turned to this page.

It must be remembered that Harry and I were sitting in this house at a time in our lives during which we were in a terrible quandary about how to reconcile our feelings for each other with the inescapable fact of the difference in our beliefs. It seemed that help and guidance would never be forthcoming. Now, having cast my eyes curiously at the printed page to which I had turned, I read the following:

> "Intreat me not to leave thee, or to return from following after thee; for whither thou goest, I will go; and where thou lodgest, I will lodge; thy people shall be my people, and thy God, my God. Where thou diest will I die, and there will I be buried; the Lord do so to me and more also, if aught but death part thee and me." *(Ruth 1:16-17)*

These brave, eternal, and uncompromising words engraved themselves upon my mind and heart so immediately and so deeply that they became a very part of me throughout that whole evening. I kept going over them, going over the resounding parade of the immortal words of those verses: ". . . thy people shall be my people, and thy God my God, where thou diest, I will die, and there will I be buried. The Lord do so to me and more also, if aught but death part thee me."

I did not know then the power of the Word. I did not know, as I later found when the Bible became my constant companion and guide, that in another part of the book these words are written:

> For the Word of God is quick and powerful, and sharper than any two-edged sword, piercing even to the dividing asunder of soul and spirit and of the joints and marrow; and is a discerner of the thoughts and intents of the heart. *(Hebrews 4:12)*

A Hand On My Shoulder

God had indeed discerned the very intents of my heart, and in His unerring wisdom deigned to reveal to me the answer to my problem. The confusion, bewilderment, and troubled sorrow of the past many months were dispelled in a moment of revelation of His holy words. It was as though a heavy cloud were lifted from the face of the sun, and I could see my path clear and straight before me. I greeted it with joy and resolution.

That evening, when Harry escorted me home to my brother's house where I was living, he again asked as he had so hopelessly done many times before, if I would marry him. Much to his astonishment and gratification, as well as to my own, the words tumbled out that had been echoing in my mind all day: ". . . thy people shall be my people, and thy God my God, where thou diest, I will die, and there will I be buried. The Lord do so to me and more also, if aught but death part thee me."

So we were engaged, and then married in the sight of God on June 15, 1920 in the Methodist Episcopal Church on Woodward Avenue at Grand Circus Park in the city of Detroit, Michigan.

Methodist Episcopal Church
Now known as the Central United Methodist Church

16

Chapter 5

Married Life

Following our wedding, the immemorial problems of a newly married couple faced us as well. My husband, being a man of modest means, had a limited bank account. So on the question of our home-to-be, he offered me the choice between a pleasant little flat, a car, and a few years of freedom, or settling down at once to buy a home. After several years of being footloose with room and board as a home base, my choice was immediate. I voted for settling down in a home and having children, of which I had always declared I wanted ten, not knowing that God one day would give me three thousand "children."

So we prepared to build and bought a lot outside the city limits. But a short time later, we were faced with tragedy. The contractor whom we had paid to build our home had absconded with our money. We were left with only a partially excavated basement and an unfinished one-car garage which had been used as a tool shed. As I look back, however, I can see the Hand of God again in guidance of my life's events. My husband and I accepted, as gratefully as we could, the fate that had befallen us, neither blaming the other. Hand in hand we moved happily into the garage, which was nothing more than a shed. A little paint and chintz, a grass rug, and a few wicker chairs with a generous mixture of love and industry, turned it into a delightful place to live. We pretended we were living in a country cabin, and indeed many of our facilities resembled such an abode. We used kerosene lamps. There was no plumbing, so water had to be carried by hand. We cooked on an oil stove and were warmed by a base burner. In the spring we wore hip boots even to the store. But we had many delightful times in our pioneering, as each pay envelope advanced us a short step to "civilization," until we had added onto our little cabin a living room, dinette, bedroom, kitchen and lavatory—even a small porch!

In the midst of exceeding happiness with my husband, for we loved as I believe few have loved, and the excitement of building a home from practically nothing, my separation from the church of my childhood weighed heavily upon me from time to time. Having been married outside of the church, all past connections had been severed. Yet I continued to hope that somehow a lifeline would be thrown to me—the missing link replaced between the church of my childhood, my relatives, and friends. In the meantime, I followed the line of least resistance, and when despair would descend upon me, the verse of Scripture which in the first place had guided me, seemed to have the power to soothe and reassure me:

> "Intreat me not to leave thee, or to return from following after me; for whither thou goest, I will go; and where thou lodgest, I will lodge; thy people shall be my people and thy God my God. Where thou diest there will I die and there will I be buried; the Lord do so to me and more also, if aught but death part thee and me."
> *(Ruth 1:16-17)*

My estrangement from my church and my God, and the separation from my own people, was the only unhappiness I had, but it was a bitter thread. I believe this suffering was one of the reasons I have appreciated my salvation so much. I knew I was lost. Perhaps that is why many do not value their salvation as I did—they never knew they were lost. If we would deal bread to the hungry, we must buy the loaf.

* * *

In our third year of marriage, our first child was on the way. On February 22, 1923, our little girl was born, whom we named Doris Patricia, (who would later change the order of her name to Patricia Doris). As I went under ether for that baby, my last thought was: "If

I die, I will open my eyes in hell." I very nearly did die. They sent for my mother, but God was merciful and spared both of our lives.

After I was up and around again, and mother had returned home, whenever I would prepare to bathe the baby, I would always put a cup of water on the chair alongside the wash bowl and christen Patricia. I had been taught that all unbaptized babies would not go to heaven but to Limbo, a place of eternal darkness. I didn't know much about christening, and I feared always that I had not done it properly, so each day I would try a different method. One day I would say the words and then pour the water. The next time, I would pour the water and afterward say the words. On a third day, I would pour the water and say the words at the same time. I venture to say that few, if any, babies have been as thoroughly christened as was mine.

Patricia was a beautiful child, and when she was five years old, we discovered she had a great talent for music. At that time and ever since, she has been a great source of enjoyment to us. I never had a little sister, and if Patricia had been a little boy, I would have been terribly disappointed for that reason. I always thank God that He gave me a little girl baby to make up for never having had a little sister. Patricia and I have always been more like sisters than mother and daughter.

When Patricia was creeping age, about Thanksgiving time when it was getting cold, we had an opportunity to sell our little cabin for the exact amount we had lost in our first transaction. So we moved into a new home—a five-room bungalow, modest but with modern conveniences. Everything was pleasant and desirable. Harry had a good position, and we had everything that a sensible person could wish for. Yet another joy was added when we found that another baby was on the way. On December 13, 1924, James Lee was born. Once again I was face to face with the church problem.

God had showered upon me love and affection. I had two beautiful children and all the worldly comfort one could ask for. Yet there was a reaching out for God in me—a spiritual hunger that needed to be fed. It was a starvation akin to acute pain and suffering in the midst of corporeal plenty. I have often thought there is a definite difference between conviction and conscience, and here was a demonstration of that philosophy. I had been instructed to believe that my Church was the Bride of Christ and to be outside of the

Catholic Church was to be outside the Bride: the answer spelled "Hell." My conscience was trained to think in those terms, and I was convinced that I was without a church and, therefore, without a God.

Conscience is a tricky thing, and often we are convicted by our conscience according to the way we have taught it to think, but the conviction of God is another story. We are convicted by the Holy Spirit according to the mind of God and Truth. If I had understood God's conviction in the beginning as I do now, I would have waited patiently and calmly for God to bring me to the place in Him that He had planned for me before the foundation of the world. But because I did not understand it, and because of the insistence of my conscience and the pressure of loved ones, I went through much needless torture and suffering. I could not know that God was leading me steadily on. I could not know that in a very short time, I would find that for which God had apprehended me when He gave me the Scripture that changed the whole trend of my life.

I could not know that I was again, after a long time of waiting, to feel once more the touch of *His Hand* on my shoulder.

Chapter 6

The Little Methodist Church

The time had now arrived when I was confronted with an inescapable problem—the Christian training of my two children. My own religious dilemma I could compromise with, but there was no procrastination possible with Patricia Doris and James Lee. The decision had to be mine. My husband did not feel the responsibility of the children's spiritual training as I did. Knowing that he would never consent to their being trained in the Catholic dogma, I made the only remaining decision—to take them to the little Methodist church in our neighborhood.

This neighborhood church had scheduled what they called a "church supper," and my husband had bought tickets for our entire family. On the designated night, we attended this supper which was held in the church basement. The women very kindly made us feel most welcome. I shall never forget how the pastor's wife took pains to convince us that our presence was indispensable to the success of the function.

We thoroughly enjoyed the evening. As we were leaving, the pastor's wife managed to leave me with the thought that if I did not come the following Sunday morning and enroll my children in Sunday school, the session could hardly go on at all. So I had little left to do but give my promise. So on that Sunday morning, we prepared ourselves carefully. I was to attend my first service in a church other than a Roman Catholic one. I delivered the children to their class held in the church basement, and then I sat waiting in the vestibule with the other mothers who had brought their children.

The morning service in this little Methodist church seemed very strange to me. I had been accustomed to the solemnity of the Mass

A Hand On My Shoulder

read in Latin, the choir singing in the same language, the incense, lighted candles on the beautiful and elaborate altars, and priests in colorful vestments. This plain, simple service seemed to me to lack the reverence and sanctity of the Catholic ritual. Yet, I could not help but take note of the sincerity of the worshippers, nor to fail to take food for my hungry soul in the reading and preaching of the Word.

Sunday after Sunday, I continued taking my children to Sunday School, sitting in the vestibule with other mothers until their class was finished. As we mothers became better acquainted, the conversation would often turn to things of God and prayer. One Sunday, one of the ladies said she felt I knew so much more about the Bible than they did and suggested that I teach them while we waited for our children, and so have our own class. I laughed and declined, explaining that I had never studied the Bible, and that what I knew I had learned only from the study of Bible history. Yet they were insistent and declared that even this knowledge was more than they possessed. So strangely I found myself, never having experienced real salvation and with no true knowledge of the Word, a Catholic who had cut ties with her faith, teaching an adult Sunday School Class in the Methodist Church!

Drawing upon the training I had received at the Women's Teachers College, I took pains in preparing the lessons, enlarging much upon the geographical and moral aspects of them. What I lacked in spiritual understanding, I compensated for with research and preparation. As I continued in the study of the Word, I began to face many truths that influenced me. Yet with typical stubbornness, when I would face the class I would tell them: "Now, you see, I was raised a Catholic and I don't believe this, but you are supposed to believe it." Their answer was always, "Well, that's fair enough with us." What we may have missed spiritually, we made up for with an education in tolerance.

My children were greatly enjoying Sunday School, and while I was not satisfied that God was wholly pleased with me, still I felt that somehow *His Hand* was drawing near to me again. We made many firm friends in the church. Our lives were enriched, and I began to feel as though we belonged. The Adult Sunday School class had grown. From the mothers' class of a few months back, it had become a real adult class.

The Little Methodist Church

Because of my study of the Word and with the influence of these new surroundings, I was going through different stages of conviction, and, of confusion. I had mixed feelings of frustration, condemnation and insecurity, of conscience and dissatisfaction, and the working of the Word. For the Lord says, "The entrance of His Word gives light," *(Psalm 119:130)*, and this light was dispelling the darkness in my soul. This meant a battle, for light and darkness can never co-exist.

* * *

One Sunday morning, a gentleman entered our class, a stranger. There was something about his bearing that made me feel undone, and I knew I could not teach that class in his presence. There was something about him that convinced me that he knew the Word and how it should be taught. So I asked him if he would teach the class. He laughed and told me I was doing very nicely, but my feeling of insufficiency was intensified. At the close of the class, he asked me why I did not want to teach that day. I had the feeling that he knew the reason. I did not know the Lord through personal knowledge; my training had only taught me a distant awareness of Him. I tried to explain this to the man, but he only seemed to think it very strange that I did not know God with a personal knowledge.

Because of a sort of inner light that I saw reflected on this man's face, and because of the quiet, calm smile that made one know he had a secret, in my vexation of spirit, I privately called him "Mr. Shiny Face." From that time on, whenever he came into my class, he always made me feel that I was talking about something of which I had no real knowledge.

On the same Sunday that Mr. Shiny Face first entered my class, our minister announced during the service that we would have a prayer meeting on Wednesday night. This term was so strange to me that when I returned home I asked my husband, "What is a prayer meeting?" He replied that he was not sure, but he supposed it was a meeting where they prayed! I determined then and there to attend this prayer meeting and see what it was all about.

When I arrived on the Wednesday evening, there were not many people present, about twenty. Our minister spoke for a few minutes from the Word. Then he gave this word of encouragement: "Now, let everyone give a sentence prayer." He tried his best to encourage

A Hand On My Shoulder

us to pray aloud. There was no response until suddenly Mr. Shiny Face arose and knelt beside his chair. He was to the rear and side of me, so I could not see him. But when he began to pray, I was enthralled. When he would pray, "Oh, God!" something inside of me seemed to tie up in knots. I had never heard such a prayer in all my life.

Because of my previous religious training, I supposed his prayer was memorized. I thought to myself, surely he has studied elocution. Such expression, such vehemence, such supplication, I had never before heard. The intonation of his voice as it rose and fell caused me to feel my insufficient and undone condition. I could feel on the one hand Hell opening for me, and on the other all Heaven trying to call to me. When he finished, his face was bathed in tears, but it had not lost any of its shine. Upon my return home, I told my husband that I had never in my life met anyone with such a memory for prayer as that man had. I was certain he must have memorized that prayer from a prayer book. I decided in my heart that I must go back the following Wednesday night and hear that prayer again.

At the next Wednesday night prayer meeting, eagerly in attendance, I marked Mr. Shiny Face's place and sat where I would be able to watch him when he prayed. When the minister again urged the rest of us to give a sentence prayer, and no one would respond, Mr. Shiny Face again arose, knelt by his chair, and began to pray. To my utter amazement, he delivered a brand new prayer. And this one seemed even more beautiful than the first, and longer as well. I was positive by this time that he must excel in intelligence, for surely no one could memorize prayers and give them with such sincerity and expression unless he were very well educated.

I attended each prayer meeting without fail from then on, and each time Mr. Shiny Face had a new prayer. Soon the minister decided to change the order of this prayer meeting. I realize now that Mr. Shiny Face's prayers were bringing God a little too close for comfort and a little beyond even our minister's understanding, so he decided he would assign different ones to deliver a prayer at each meeting instead of calling for volunteers.

I knew that one day my turn would come, and I made up my mind that I would excel Mr. Shiny Face. Therefore, I wrote and rewrote a beautiful prayer copied out of a prayer book, adding to it my own ingenuity until I was sure my prayer passed his in eloquence.

The Little Methodist Church

But when it came to memorizing it, I could not manage it. So I took a piece of paper cut to the size of the hymn book, wrote the prayer on it, and pasted it in the book.

When it came to be my turn to lead in prayer, I was thus prepared. I told everyone to close their eyes and bow their heads. But one lady that I knew, who was full of mischief, had evidently guessed my secret. When everyone else had bowed their heads, I looked up and saw her peeking. I stared her directly in the eye and said, "Everyone, put down your heads and close your eyes!" Then I began to read my prayer with all the ardor and expression of which I was capable. But as I closed my prayer with what I thought was great success, I looked up and saw them all peeking at me! You may conclude with what chagrin and embarrassment I remember my prayer, particularly in view of my present conviction that true prayer comes spontaneously and from the heart, not from literary invention and memory.

As I look back to this and other experiences, I see the mercy and the gentleness of God as He leads His dear children along. Surely what the Psalmist says is true: "He leadeth us beside still waters, and maketh us to lie down in green pastures." Surely, "He does spread a table before us." And, His "goodness and mercy shall follow you all the days of your life."[1]

I did not know that in just a very short time, I would again be feeling *His Hand* on my shoulder—hearing His voice and seeing the vision that brought me God's own salvation.

---

[1] Myrtle has personalized these words of Scripture. See Psalm 23

Chapter 7

The Drifting Ship Finds A Pilot

I was enjoying the associations I had made at the little church in our neighborhood, but it was a social satisfaction. At the same time there were periods of depression and a heaviness of spirit which I could not understand. With hindsight I recognize these disturbances to have been a turmoil of my soul caused by the convicting of the Holy Spirit and the alteration of my past beliefs. My study of the Word in preparation for my teaching of the Sunday School class was doing the work in me that was finally to bring about my conversion. A long-closed window was being opened in my heart, a long-drawn blind raised.

One day an odd conversation occurred between our pastor, Mr. Shiny Face, and me. The pastor asked about my spiritual progress, and I replied that I was disturbed and in a deep quandary, not knowing in truth what was wrong with me. Mr. Shiny Face turned to the pastor and asked: "Parson, don't you know what ails this woman?" But the minister did not reply. As I walked home through the night, I pondered on the things which troubled me. Not long after this conversation, the momentous day arrived when I received the revelation that calmed my troubled heart and changed the course of my life.

* * *

On a certain Sunday our church was without a minister. Our pastor, along with all the other ministers, was away attending an

The Drifting Ship Finds A Pilot

annual ministerial conference. Although our pastor was away, we still had our regular Sunday School hour. Afterward we gathered in the main auditorium. It was church time, but there was to be no regular service; instead different local ministers would take turns in speaking briefly. Later the thought turned to the coming of a new minister for our church after the conference.

There was a considerable divergence of opinion as to the type of minister who would best suit the needs of the church. Some thought the pastor should be one who would be adapted to the older members of the congregation. Others thought he should be attuned to the thinking of the young people. There were those who felt the new minister should devote his entire time to his calling, and then those who believed a part-time minister was sufficient.

This frank discussion of the qualifications and selection of a pastor horrified me with its seeming lack of reverence for a servant of God. I had been accustomed to having a priest for a minister, one selected and sent to a parish by the Catholic hierarchy. The congregation would accept their choice without question and in the spirit of reverence and obedience. This first experience of a church membership selecting their clergyman according to his characteristics and suitability to their special needs seemed to me as bad as bartering for a worldly possession, hiring a new employee, or voting for a political candidate. It was to be the people's choice, not God's. There was no prayer offered for His guidance in the selection.

As I sat there, greatly agitated and meditating upon the strangeness of the congregation's action, once more I felt the *Hand* upon my shoulder. I heard the Voice of the Almighty sound clearly in my heart, and this is what He said: "Tell them, it is not a minister they need to seek; they need to seek Me."

I was frightened, for though I had many times before felt the touch of *His Hand*, I had never previously heard *His Voice*. I trembled with a pounding heart until I thought everyone around me must hear it. I could not rise to my feet. I was filled with a great consternation. But again, insistently, the *Voice* echoed in my heart: "Tell them, it is not a minister they need to seek; they need to seek Me."

With renewed fear and terror I clutched tightly to my chair. I was certain everyone had heard what I had heard. Yet I could find neither strength nor courage to obey the command, until for the third time with unmistakable force and authority, the *Voice* rang through my inner being, "TELL THEM!"

Suddenly I found myself on my feet. Though I could scarcely find my voice, I managed to falter, "He said, it is not a minister you need to seek; you need to seek HIM!"

In a moment, so fraught with the power and omnipotence of God were the words He had spoken through my unsure throat. Suddenly everyone present found a place at the altar. I had never in the time I had attended this little church seen the altar used in this way. In fact, I knew nothing of the "altar call." I had never witnessed one. As I recall now, it still seems strange that all of us, everyone, should have moved as a single being to the altar. Some were praying, others singing as God visited His people.

At the altar myself, it was as though I were alone there, unmindful of anyone near me. I was in the grasp of the Holy Spirit, pouring out to Him all the transgressions of my life—my headache, my heartbreak. I didn't know how to ask God to save me. I knew not the words or the way. I didn't ask Him to convert me or to be born again, I only said:

> "God, if there is a God, as I have always been taught to believe, and if you could forgive me, if in your great storehouse of mercy you have mercy enough to extend to me, if you could give me peace and the assurance that I will not be sent to Hell, but achieve Heaven, then I will give to you the rest of my life."

At that instant, something happened in my soul. The burden that was on my heart for years was rolled away and into that heart came a deep, settled peace. The fear of Hell was removed from me and the surety of coming into the atonement of God filled my whole being. That beautiful assurance of meeting God at the end of the road and knowing that Heaven is my eternal home has never left me. I am reminded of the lines of this hymn by Isaac Watts:

> At the Cross, at the Cross,
> Where I first saw the light,
> And the burden of my heart rolled away.

The Drifting Ship Finds A Pilot

> It was there by faith,
> I received my sight,
> And now I am happy all the day.

Note: Patricia Beall Gruits remembers this day clearly. "Mother took Jim and I by the hand and rushed us the two blocks home. We burst into the house and she called to my dad, "Harry, I'm not going to Hell." Dad responded, "Who said you were?" Mother answered, "I've known it since we have been married."

The natural thing for one in love to do is to try to express that love in doing things for the object of one's devotion. After I was saved, a great zeal to work for the Lord seemed to possess me and the desire to please Him. At that time, I was not aware that there was any place for a woman in the ministry, but I set out on my own to do everything my hands found to do. I began to give myself to prayer—praying for people who needed the same kind of peace I had needed, telling them how I had met God, and how wonderful He was to deliver me. I set out to work for God and to do everything I could that others might find Him and through Him have peace.

I confess my efforts were blundering and feeble, but I continued to try to keep my word to God who had shown me such merciful favor. I believe the reason so many people do not appreciate God's peace and salvation as they should is because they never fully realized the torment of knowing they were lost and hell bound. I had known I was without hope, and when God in His mercy gave me hope, peace, and the joy of His salvation, nothing in the world could be as wonderful.

The members of my Bible class, with which I continued, realized that something had happened to me. They expressed a desire to have the same experience themselves. Often the teaching in the class would be interrupted while someone inquired about salvation. Some, who had been saved and had already known the Way but had not lived it, were challenged by my experience to begin anew. Our class became alive with knowledge of the Lord and an eagerness to serve Him. Always their testimony was the same. They had been inspired by the change in my own life and ministry. So we continued serving the Lord in ministering to the needs of others, both temporal and spiritual, in accordance with this passage in James: "Even so faith, if it has not works, is dead, being alone. Yea, a man may say, thou hast faith, and I have works; shew me thy faith without thy works, and I will shew thee my faith by my works." *(James 2:17-18)*

    I love the Lord with all my heart, all my life, and all my strength. Whatever I have is His. He can place His Hand on me or anything I possess. It is His! When I left the altar that Sunday morning, I did not, as always before, voyage forth alone. One went with me who guided my every step. I was no longer a ship adrift upon a lost and lonely sea. I had taken on a Pilot—One who had His Hand upon the helm and was directing the ship surely, peacefully, into the sheltered waters of a safe harbor.

Chapter 8

The Great Physician, The Great Deliverer

For some, the way to God is easier than for others. A simplicity of heart, a singleness of soul, and a life free of complications and perplexities help to make the way straight and smooth for such fortunate ones. Yet far from regretting the obstacles and the deviousness of the path that made my journey difficult, I thank God that He did not make the way too easy for me. As the stormy voyage makes the home port more beautiful and welcome for the sailor, so the traveler appreciates refuge to a greater degree when the highway has been rocky and tortuous.

God was surely leading me on, surely and safely, though slowly, past the dangers of the steep and dangerous road to His grace. As I look back, I can see the pattern from the very beginning. From the very first work of conviction of the Holy Spirit that I ever felt in my heart, through days of trials and afflictions, to the present day. I find all of His works are glorious and "all things work together for good to them that love God, to them who are called according to his purpose." *(Rom. 8:28)*

Often we view the pattern of our life from the underside. We see there a tangled mass of colored threads and knots that are seemingly without plan or purpose, leading in all directions and emerging at random from many places—a meaningless and hopeless jumble. But from God's side, we can see the beautiful embroidery of a life's pattern as it is woven by Him, an elaborate and orderly network of threads of all colors, every design different, yet all with singleness of plan and purpose, which in the end completes His design.

A Hand On My Shoulder

Perhaps it is the Lily of the Valley or the Rose of Sharon which emerges from His needle or some other picture of perfect symmetry and beauty. But we can be sure that every thread, every stitch, every tear, and pain has a meaning. They are working into an exquisite pattern, a glorious wedding garment for that one who can stand quiet and patient, and let Him do His work.

The days that followed my conversion were glorious and, at the same time, terrible days—glorious through the realization of sins which had been forgiven, the reveling in His presence, His nearness, and His love, but terrible because of the beckoning of the Spirit into uncharted waters and unmapped roads. *His Voice* spoke softly, encouragingly: "Come a little farther. Let Me take you into My chambers." As a child who had never explored the chambers of God, there was within me a longing and wanting. At the same time there was a fear and a drawing back, the mixture of emotions which besets those stepping into the unknown and unfamiliar. Such a mixture of emotions was mine that I was confused and bewildered. I did not know truly who I was, or what this new-found salvation was leading me to, or what it would take me away from.

But loving Him supremely, I could only say: "You lead me, Father, for I have no other guide." And so, step by step, moment by moment, He drew me out and on. Though I feared my unfitness and readiness for the place He had prepared for me, I was ever conscious and trustful of His loving Presence and His guiding Hand.

* * *

About this time, the goiter which I had suffered with from childhood became active. It became toxic and had begun to spread poisons through my entire system. I was in very poor health and was constrained to visit the University Hospital in Ann Arbor, Michigan for some metabolism tests. From these and other tests, the doctors deduced that I needed to enter the hospital for a thyroid operation. I had completed my tests on a Friday and was committed to enter the hospital on Sunday. At that time, although I had already learned a great deal about Him and His ways, I had not yet heard about divine healing.

On Saturday, the day before I was to submit to the knife, a Christian worker came to see me at my home. I had never met her

The Great Physician, The Great Deliverer

before and knew nothing about her faith or her religious affiliation. After a short chat, she commenced to tell me that it had come to her knowledge that I was ill and suffering greatly. She assured me that if she prayed for me, and if I would believe that the Lord would Himself heal me, that I would not need to have the operation.

We had a bedroom just off the living room, and she suggested that we go in there, kneel together at the side of the bed, and she would pray for me. I assented, and we fell on our knees in the calm and quiet of the little room. As she began to pray, I suddenly became aware that something was happening in my throat and neck, an indescribable sensation which frightened me badly. In my fear of the unknown and unfamiliar, I begged that she pray no more, that since my plans were made to go to the hospital, I would continue as I had planned. I was actually petrified with fear. I was sure that this woman must be a witch! I have often thought since then of the discouragement and disappointment which this good woman must have felt at my deliberate refusal of God's power and grace, which might have been imparted to me through her.

I knew nothing at that time of praying in the Spirit or of the power of God, even though I had the experience of being saved by it. But I have learned since then that there are many of God's servants who have been elected by Him to receive the gift of faith and healing. Would that more of us could bring ourselves to take advantage of this great gift. As I look back upon this experience, I am now sure that if I had believed, if in spite of my fear I had trusted the powerful healing hand of God, that I would have been spared the awful ordeal of this operation.

* * *

The following day, Sunday, a few friends from the little Methodist Church visited to pray with me before I was to leave for the hospital. How well I remember that day! To me, it has always been one of the greatest moments of my life. My modest home was indeed Holy Ground. We were all broken in His presence. I left my home for the hospital fortified with renewed faith in God and in my salvation, for I was sure that He had heard the prayers of these good friends to bring me back to rear my family. My fear and trepidation were dispelled, and I placed my faltering hand in His with utmost trust and confidence, knowing that He would bring me through the darkness out into the light again to take up, with renewed health, my travels toward His goal.

* * *

"Many are the afflictions of the righteous: but God delivereth him out of them all…" *(Ps. 34:19)*

"The angel of the Lord encampeth round about them that fear Him and delivereth them…" *(Ps. 34:7)*

These words of Scripture were proved to me in the days that followed. My operation was a serious one, and I hovered between two worlds for many days. There is a time of the night, before day-break, when the ill and suffering are conscious of a heavy darkness; when it seems that the powers of evil and death are fighting for the patient's mind and soul, spirit and body; when one wonders if he will see the light of another day. So it was with me in the days that followed my operation.

I remember one early morning just before dawn, when it seemed my body was being riven asunder by pain. I was powerless to move in anywise. Suddenly at the peak of my torture, a little nurse entered my room. She silently slipped her hands under my back and lifted me up into a comfortable position. She seemed to know just where to place her hands, just where the pain and distress centered, and where release was most needed. I said to her wonderingly, "My, you know just where it hurts, don't you?"

But she only smiled and left as quietly as she had come. After that night, she was my constant and regular visitor in the terrible hour just before sunrise. I always knew when to expect her—at the moment when the pain was about to become unbearable. Her hair was so fair, her skin so translucent, and her uniform so snowy white, that in my mind I called her "the little white nurse." As time passed, I grew ever more thankful and grateful for her countless kindnesses and for the love and mercy she showed me. I looked forward to her nightly advent with great eagerness and expectance.

Then one morning, after she had as usual made me comfortable and soothed my pain, she whispered into my ear. I could feel her breath upon my ear and neck as she said, "Now dear, you are going

The Great Physician, The Great Deliverer

to begin to get well. Your temperature is going to go down now, and you are going to recover."

A little later on this same morning, another nurse came in and asked me how I was feeling. As she prepared to take my temperature, I told her how the little white nurse had told me that my temperature would go down, and that I was going to recover. She asked, "What little white nurse? What did she look like?" I described her as best I could and told her she was the one who came to me every morning before daybreak to comfort and encourage me.

The nurse took my temperature wordlessly and left hurriedly, only to return in a few minutes with another nurse. Again she asked me to describe the little white nurse's appearance, words, and actions. I recounted how wonderful the little white nurse was to me, what she did and said. In a moment or two they left and came back again. This time they came with a doctor who also asked to hear the story.

By now I knew that something was amiss. I hoped and prayed that I had said or done nothing that would get "my" nurse in trouble. They left the room without comment. Later that day I was informed that my temperature was going down, and that I was so much improved I would be moved to a four-bed ward. I remonstrated, wanting to know if the little white nurse would be on duty in that part of the hospital. For some reason I could not account for, I felt that my very life was in her hands.

The nurse who was my informant very kindly sat down near me. She told me there was no nurse on that floor of the description I had given, nor ever had been. She suggested with great consideration that my comforter in the long night's reaches might have been a heavenly visitor. I don't know whether she believed her own words or was merely trying to quietly comfort me. But as I continued to regain my strength, I knew beyond the shadow of a doubt that my visitor was indeed of celestial origin. The Lord in His grace and mercy had sent His angel to minister unto me.

* * *

The patients in the four-bed ward to which I had been removed were very ill. I, too, became so weak that it frightened me. I thought, if I had not died before, I surely would now. The atmosphere was

A Hand On My Shoulder

most depressing. The patients suffered visibly and audibly—some moaning, some groaning, others nauseated with pain.

It was about half-past ten in the morning. I had been made comfortable after having been moved. As was the habit of the staff, they cut a four-fold gauze into pieces and gave one to each of us as a handkerchief. Because of my fear and nervousness, I was perspiring and weeping. I took the piece of gauze I had been given and tried to shake it out so that I could wipe away my tears and sweat. Self-pity had overcome me, and I was beginning to give way to my sorrow and terror. Then suddenly, through my tears, and in the midst of the misty folds of the white gauze, I saw the face of the Agonized Christ!

In terrifying detail, I beheld the very physical marks of His suffering, of the futility of men who did not know Him. There, in very truth, was the thorn-scarred brow, the torn bleeding flesh where the thorns had pressed. There was the dust of the road, clotted and matted in the open wounds of his forehead. I saw how the blood and sweat flowed down his brow and into his eyes, which were swollen and blackened from blows and suffering. The same blood, perspiration, and dust mingled now with his tears, flowed down his cheeks into his beard, which had been roughly plucked from the tender flesh, leaving it ragged and bleeding. I saw his nostrils, distended and discolored from the blows which had struck him—the lips swollen and cracked. Yet through those lips, with those darkened and puffed eyelids, He smiled at me. It was a smile of supreme encouragement He gave me. I thought and remembered; ". . . yet He opened not His mouth . . . as a sheep before her shearers is dumb."*(Isa. 53:7)*

When the vision passed, I felt such great shame at my small and selfish complaining, my distrust of His promise that I would recover, even after hearing the assurance from the mouth of one of His witnesses. I turned over on my side and said as I faced the wall: "Forgive me, Lord. You will hear no further word of complaint from my lips. And if you will let me live and return to my family, I will go back as Your witness."

I am neither artist nor poet, but if I could paint, I would be able to reproduce every detail, every line of the face I saw that day, for it has burned itself into my mind in such a way that it would be easy for me to draw it from memory. But since I cannot paint, I pray that this

The Great Physician, The Great Deliverer

picture in words will stir the hearts of all who read it, that they may see again and know again how truly Jesus paid the terrible debt of sin for you and me.

* * *

In due time, I was dismissed from the hospital. However, I was not yet completely well. The incision continued to drain, and they had put a tube in my throat to draw off the serum. The incision, striving to heal, troubled and pained me greatly. Naturally I came home from the hospital unable to take up my household duties or care for my family. After a period, we all became very discouraged, as there seemed to be no progress in my healing.

My brother took me back to the hospital to see if there wasn't something, anything, they could do to help me. We were told by a kindly physician that they had done all they could do for me. He suggested that if I knew how to pray that I take this means of seeking recovery. Neither my brother nor I appreciated this advice from a physician. We felt it was, as they say, a "brush-off." However, after I returned home, in the days that followed, the awful distress drove me to my knees. I pleaded with God for mercy, for it seemed I obtained no rest by day or night. But man's extremity is God's opportunity. In just a matter of days, God would reveal to me the good news that Jesus heals today as He did when He walked the shores of Galilee. I was about to be made known the truth of the words of Scripture which so encouragingly say: "Jesus Christ the same, yesterday, and today, and forever." *(Heb. 13:8)*

Chapter 9

The Healing Complete

"The Lord directs the steps of the godly." *(Ps. 37:23 AMP)*

In the great economy of God, I found that the actions of a godly man or woman are indeed designed and directed by the Almighty. I was to learn that God has a method of deputizing certain of His children to do His work in a way I had never before known or suspected.

I have related the story of my agony and despair in the hospital following a serious operation, and how my hopelessness was converted into the conviction of life and redemption from pain by the ministrations of a heavenly visitor. Now I will continue with the details of the way in which her earthly counterpart, a modest and simple living woman, brought about a deliverance that was all the more miraculous, because it was affected by what seemed to be a human agency, but in truth was a deputy of the Lord.

When I was discharged from the hospital in Ann Arbor, I remained far from well. My incision failed to heal properly. I was in constant and continuing pain, unable to assume my normal home duties. There seemed no progress whatever in my healing. Even my physician confessed that the only course he could recommend was prayer. I prayed. Yet there seemed no diminution, no surcease from the distress and misery that tortured me. The physical pain, the discouragement, and the constant realization that my family and my home were being deprived of my attention overwhelmed me. I did not know which way to turn. Again as I had experienced in the hospital during the days just following my operation, I was close to despair. Yet in this seeming crisis of my life, when there was no healing for me, God was setting in operation the wheels of His great soul-saving machinery.

* * *

In our concern with our own pursuits, our own problems and pains, we give little thought to the problems and pursuits of our fellow man. The all-seeing vision is God's power alone. Even a hundred yards from one's own dwelling, a story may be being enacted of equal interest to our own. Without our being aware, the current of life flows in many small rivulets to make the great stream that rushes past the sight of the Lord.

At this time, when I was concentrated on my own dilemma to the exclusion of all other concerns, there was a little woman as unknown to me as one on the other side of the world. She was involved in a problem of her own—a happier problem, but one no less important to her. At the moment of which I write, she was having a conversation with her husband regarding the purchase of a new home. Her husband had a very good position, affording him ample remuneration. He was advising his good wife to go out in search of a new modern home with contemporary conveniences more suited to their present income than the modest home they had purchased in less prosperous days on the east side of the city. His wife thanked him for his consideration of her; but being a Christian and knowing of the leadings of the Lord, she answered with a mental reservation that she would hold it before the Lord.

The following day she took a list from a newspaper where homes for sale were being advertised. She laid her hands upon the pages of this newspaper and prayed after this fashion:

> "Now, Lord, You know that I have given you my life to be Your witness. I am in no way interested in what kind of house I will buy, except it should be where You wish me to labor for You. Place me, dear Lord, where I can be of service to Your souls and of help in building Your kingdom. I will run my finger

down the columns of this page, and where You shall stop my finger, there will I go to seek my future home."

And thus she did. When she had reached a certain advertisement, she felt suddenly arrested of the Lord. After examining the details of the advertisement, she took her hat and purse and started out for the address mentioned in the paper.

It was in a part of the city with which she was not acquainted. Accompanied by the real estate agent who had been commissioned to sell the property, she mounted the steps and opened the door of the house. As she did so, a cloud of gnats flew up into their faces. The fumes of hops, beer, and liquor rose to meet them from the basement, where there was a still. A more discouraging reception would be hard to imagine. Yet, the little woman knew that for His own reasons, God had directed her footsteps to this house. It was filthy, run down, and anything but the modern home her husband had suggested that she find. But with the wisdom only God can give, she refrained from telling him about it until she had it cleaned, fumigated, painted, and papered. Only then did she take her husband to the home she had purchased. He said, "Well, it isn't modern, but it is very clean and homey." He was satisfied because it was what she wanted, and she was satisfied.

This house was directly across the street from where I lived.

* * *

Soon after this couple had moved in, this godly woman heard of my serious plight. Immediately she came to visit me and to tell me with unwavering conviction that "Jesus heals." I could neither receive her strange testimony, nor her assertion that she had been healed of cancer and a tumor and was now a well woman. I had never heard of such a thing at that time. I could not be sure that she was telling the truth, until I challenged her to take me to the one who had prayed for her.

But the challenge merely delighted her. She expressed herself as not only eager to take me, but also to help me ready myself for the journey and to obtain a car to transport me. Now I was face-to-face with my own challenge—the decision to take or refrain from this momentous step. I did not know that God had moved this woman there for me, for my healing and the ministry that lay ahead. This woman had no recommendation other than her great and unquestioning faith in God, a childlike faith, a faith that knew no defeat.

On our way, she told me she was taking me to the Reverend McCaulden of the Christian Missionary Alliance Church on the eastside of the city. She shared how he had prayed for her, and she knew he would be delighted to pray for me as well. So she took me to this dear saint of God, who prayed a simple prayer of faith over me and anointed me with oil in the Name of the Lord. He told me, "It would be done according to the Word of God." He also told me that whatever my symptoms might be, and however much I might suffer after the prayer, not to regard it—for these would be lying symptoms. He said, "They that observe lying vanities forsake their own mercy." *(Jonah 2:8)* He told me that I must not believe the pain of the symptoms, but only the Word of God.

Such was my conviction, trust, and belief in the truth of this holy man that I had not one instant's doubt in his words. For three days and nights after my return home, though I went through the tortures of the damned, wild with pain and with aggravation on every side, I only replied to the questions and concern of my husband and my friends: "These are but lying symptoms. I am healed!"

And at the end of the third day, the symptoms disappeared. There was no more draining from the incision in my neck. The incision itself began to heal, and to the utter amazement of my family, my friends, and myself, I found that I was "every whit whole." Now I realize that it is easy for people to believe that God healed in the Old Testament when He said, ". . . for I am the Lord that healeth thee." *(Exodus 15:26)* And, it is easy to believe that Jesus healed when He walked the shores of Galilee. We submit with easy credence to the records of healing in the Early Church as recorded in the Bible, but it is difficult for us to believe that Jesus heals today, a man or woman who may live upon our street or indeed our own selves. But, Jesus Christ is "the same yesterday, and today, and forever." *(Hebrews 13:8)*

* * *

A Hand On My Shoulder

The little woman whom God had moved across a city, to a strange place and a forbidding home to lead me to this wonder, was named Nelly Williams. She was a godly woman, full of faith and good works. I pray that this memorial of her faith shall challenge those who read this account. The faith of Sister Williams and her life of prayer prepared the ground work in my Christian life for my future ministry. That is why I say; "The steps of a godly man or a godly woman are truly directed by the Lord."

Chapter 10

Prepared For A New Baptism

After my last appointment with the doctor in the hospital, I was instructed to avoid all persons, places or things that might cause excitement. My physical condition was such that complete peace and quiet was deemed necessary to my recovery. But as man proposes, God disposes. During the next few weeks, I was to experience events of a most disturbing nature. Yet their significance was such as to affect the rest of my life in God's work and my own salvation.

These events began with a strange physical sensation, somewhat akin to a chill, but yet without a feeling of cold. It was the same sensation we speak of as "goose pimples." It lasted for two days and two nights. By the second night, my reaction had become almost a shaking, so violent that I felt constrained to get up from bed so as not to disturb my husband. I slept the remainder of that night in a chair. I did not know then that this was a preparation by God for an important spiritual anointing. I thought I must surely be getting influenza or ague. I had no other way to account for the continuous trembling and shaking, a manifestation which I thought, of course, had a physical origin.

On the morning of the third day, Mrs. Williams, the woman who had been moved by the Lord to live across the street from my home, sent a note saying she was going downtown to a church to sew for the poor. She wanted to know if I would like to go with her. My heart was struck, because it was the first realization that anyone in the city was so poor that others had to sew for them. Our neighborhood was one in which everyone seemed to be getting along very nicely. I knew very little about the less fortunate parts of the city. I had never known that people were in that condition or I would have done

A Hand On My Shoulder

something before. I answered saying that I certainly would be happy to accompany her.

I had two children to get ready besides myself, so we hurried. Mrs. Williams brought along the two young daughters of her husband's nephew whom she was rearing. It was quite a journey for the six of us. We took three different street cars to get to the first Foursquare Gospel Church[2] in the city of Detroit, at Third and Warren.

There I met a group of consecrated women who met every Thursday to sew for the poor, to hear the Word of God, and to go out and work in the slums, carrying food and clothing to the penniless and ministering to the needy. Still other groups went to the hospitals and jails, winning souls, comforting and healing the sick, and carrying on the work that Jesus began.

At this time I was still a member of the Methodist Church, but never before or since have I ever met a group of people so fully consecrated to the work of the Lord. Nor have I ever seen love so manifested and expressed as I did in the Foursquare Church. These were truly days of heaven on earth. Every stitch that was put into these garments was sewn with a prayer, asking God that whoever received the garment would someday, somewhere along the way, be another soul for Him.

* * *

When lunch time came (a very meager luncheon consisting of two tablespoons of stew, a slice of bread and a cup of tea, just enough to sustain us until we reached home), we would all stand and take hold of each other's hands. We would sing the Doxology, praising God for His goodness and mercy to the children of men. While singing the Doxology, suddenly I again felt the sensation I had been experiencing for the last two days and nights. The woman next to

---

[2] "The Foursquare Church is a Pentecostal denomination that resulted from the dynamic evangelistic ministry of Aimee Semple McPherson, who opened the historic Angelus Temple on Jan. 1, 1923. Foursquare derives its name from what McPherson called the Foursquare Gospel: Jesus is the Savior, Jesus is the Healer, Jesus is the Baptizer of the Holy Spirit, Jesus is the Soon-Coming King." www.foursquare.org

Prepared For A New Baptism

me felt what I felt. She said to me afterward, "Have you ever received the Baptism of the Holy Ghost?"

I replied, yes, that I was sure I had. Of course, she knew that I had not. So she asked me if I had ever spoken in another tongue. I again replied, "Oh yes." For I had studied four years of Latin and two years of German, and I supposed that was what she was speaking of.

However, she was aware that I had misunderstood, so she asked me to attend the service that night to hear Howard Mitchell, an evangelist, speak on the Baptism of the Holy Ghost. I answered that I would do my best to come, whereupon she urged me not to miss it under any circumstances as she was convinced the Lord wanted me to hear his message. I had no conception of what she was talking about or why she should think it so important that I hear this message. But on the way home, Mrs. Williams also encouraged me to return to the Foursquare Church that evening and said she would be glad to go with me.

After wrestling four little children on and off three street cars during the city's rush hour, getting home, preparing dinner and washing the dishes afterward, I surely did not feel like making another trip downtown that night. However, God had given Mrs. Williams a very persevering nature. Since she had decided I was going to go, there was very little I could do about it. Half convinced, I mentioned to my husband that Mrs. Williams felt this man was going to speak on something very outstanding, and she was urging me to go back and hear him. My husband replied that if I would really like to go, he would stay with the children.

So I went and sat through the sermon of this fine evangelist. But not one word of what he was saying did I comprehend. In fact, I was bored to tears because I could not follow his line of reasoning, though I am sure now that he spoke very well, since everyone was thrilled with his message. My understanding, however, was so darkened I could not comprehend the light.

Following the service, I was anxious to go home for I was tired, but Mrs. Williams insisted that we go up to the "120 Room."[3] I

---

[3] This "120 Room" was where people prayed to receive the Baptism of the Holy Spirit. The "120" refers to the number of believers/disciples who were gathered in an upper room on the Day of Pentecost when they received the Gift of the Holy Spirit. *(Acts 2)*

pleaded weariness, that I was too tired even to climb the stairs, but she was adamant.

I found the room to be a large prayer room, containing a few people on their knees beseeching God. At this time, I again began to feel the strange trembling sensation. It grew in violence and so weakened me that I found myself prostrate before God and without the strength to rise. I realized afterward that I was resisting the Holy Spirit, but at that time I did not understand. Summoning all my physical resources, I continued to resist until I was able to leave the room. Accompanied by Mrs. Williams, I fled from the building just as rapidly as I possibly could.

It was not until we had boarded the street car that I realized I had left a brand new pair of expensive gloves up in the prayer room. Mrs. Williams was elated when I discovered my loss and insisted that we return for them. But I said with determination, "Oh, no! I am not going back in that room anymore." I had never experienced anything like the sensation I had gone through in that room, and I was just plain frightened. But Mrs. Williams was very wise. She ceased insisting on our returning, and did not attempt to explain anything to me. She held her peace, and we had very little conversation on the streetcar ride home.

But that night, I again arose from my bed and spent the night in a chair. The shaking and trembling that encompassed my entire body had increased until I was filled with alarm. It was the agony before the revelation. On the very next morning, as I shall explain, I received the full understanding of my experiences of the several preceding days. I was granted a glimpse into the intent of the Almighty that revealed a long vista into the future of my work in His name.

Chapter 11

A Personal Pentecost

In humble thanks and wonder, I often reflect that God in His goodness and mercy has seen fit to give me the grace of many revelations. Since the day as a little girl when I first felt the *Hand* on my shoulder, the Almighty has given me several brief glimpses into His plan for me, and my modest work in His vineyard. But few "liftings of the veil" have been as awe-inspiring as the morning following the events at the Foursquare Gospel Church—my prostration in the "120 Room."

For some days, I had been filled with a strange trembling sensation, a kind of spiritual premonition of some great event to come. That night I again experienced a trembling so violent that I spent yet another night in a chair beside my bed so that I would not disturb my husband.

The next morning at six o'clock, after my husband had left for work and before the children had risen for school, I went into the kitchen. It was in the fall of the year and, the house being chilly, I lighted the gas oven. I placed my Bible on a chair and knelt down on the floor before it to pray and study the Word. This was a regular procedure with me, to spend a short time in worship and meditation in the silence and peace of the quiet house before the bustle of the day began.

I had found it very difficult to understand the Word and could not seem to make head nor tail of it, as the saying goes. I had been asking God if there were not a key to the Scriptures, some other way to understand it. I was bewildered at my own lack of perception, since being of moderate intelligence, I had always been able to understand other books. I was at this time slowly beginning to realize that there must be some other way of understanding what we read other than through the intellect.

I did not know then that this other way of understanding was the way of the Spirit, the Paraclete, the Giver of Light, who would lead us into all truth. On this morning, as I knelt on the kitchen floor before my Bible, I was baptized in the Holy Spirit and began to speak in other tongues—a language I had never in my life learned or even heard. Suddenly there was a great rushing wind that filled the house. The windows and the doors seemed to fly open simultaneously. I received the sensation of the cloven or cleaving tongue. My tongue began to cleave to the roof of my mouth with such rapidity that my speech was changed, and I was speaking words of the Spirit: "He that speaketh in an unknown tongue speaketh not unto men, but unto God: for no man understandeth him; howbeit in the spirit he speaketh mysteries." *(1 Corinthians 14:2)*

For some moments the power and anointing of God covered and filled me with the most poignant sensation. When this feeling had begun to subside somewhat, I glanced involuntarily into the Bible on the chair before me; and there I read:

> And when the day of Pentecost was fully come, they were all with one accord in one place. And suddenly there came a sound from heaven as of a rushing mighty wind, and it filled all the house where they were sitting. And there appeared unto them cloven tongues like as of fire, and it sat upon each of them. And they were all filled with the Holy Ghost, and began to speak with other tongues, as the Spirit gave them utterance. *(Acts 2:1-4)*

I realized then with a great feeling of awe that something supernatural had just happened to me. But I was confused and bewildered at this very strange occurrence and did not know what to do about it or where to place it. I realized I was in need of counsel from someone whose understanding of such things might be greater than mine, so I determined to seek out such counsel.

At the time, I was still attending the Methodist Church in our neighborhood. When it was daylight and I had gotten the children off to school, I dressed and went to the Methodist preacher's home

A Personal Pentecost

and told him what had happened to me that morning. God witnessed to this elderly Methodist minister, Brother Colling, a minister of the old school in Methodism, and with great kindness he said to me: "My dear, you have received something from God, and I am sure that in the days to come God is going to use you to build His church and to bring in His kingdom."

He encouraged me with many wise and thoughtful words. He also warned me that there was undoubtedly persecution ahead for me, but no matter what that persecution might be, I was always to remember that God Himself had done His work in me and what God had begun, He was able to finish. I did not then understand how anyone would be persecuted over anything that God did. I felt that the tribulations of the early Christians who had suffered through the profession of God's grace belonged to the centuries of the past. But I was not left very long in the dark, for when God works, all the powers of Hell are stirred in rebellion.

I was filled with a great zeal, which unfortunately was not matched with great knowledge, but I did not leave a stone unturned until I had told everyone of my acquaintance of the wonder God had worked in my life. The days that immediately followed my baptism in the Holy Ghost were wonderful—and terrible. The Sunday School class which I was teaching began to increase in attendance and spirituality. Many were saved and continued to be saved right in the class. Seven persons received the Baptism of the Holy Ghost in prayer meetings outside the church.

All these things, of course, were done in ignorance, for I supposed that all people who were not Roman Catholics were Protestant Christians, of the same faith with basically the same dogma and interpretation of the Scriptures. I did not know there were differences in theological philosophy but believed that names like Methodist and Baptist were just different names for the same basic belief, like the names of the different Catholic churches which would be named after the various saints and titles of God. I was convinced that all Protestant churches, whatever their names, all believed in the same way and were of the same fundamental faith. So I felt that when I taught the Bible, I was doing no trespassing. I believed that the Bible was the standard of faith for all Christians, and they were never able to convince me differently because they were Methodists.

A Hand On My Shoulder

Though many tried to show me the difference in approach to God of the various sects of Protestantism, I could not conceive that there should be different roads, different approaches to the one God. I still felt with great firmness that the Bible was the one standard of faith for all Christians, so I found salvation in the Bible a genuine experience, with the Spirit witnessing with one's own spirit that one became a child of God. So my face was set to declare the whole counsel of God.

Chapter 12

I Deliver My First Sermon

Immediately after the awesome experience of being baptized in the Holy Spirit, I began a weekly prayer meeting and Bible study class in my own home among my neighbors. However, this project did not last very long. Many who were Christians longer than I seemed to resent a novice telling them things they had never before seen or heard, making it very difficult for them to receive and believe. Yet we always remained friends and at various times during the succeeding years, different ones in the group would declare that they were proud and happy that we had continued "in the Way."

At this time the Great Depression had arrived. So besides teaching a Bible class in the Methodist Church, and then in an interdenominational work, we set ourselves about feeding the hungry and clothing the poor among those families who were feeling the pinch. We embraced this verse found in the book of *James*: "Pure religion and undefiled before God and the Father is this, to visit the fatherless and widows in their affliction, and keep himself unspotted from the world." *(James 1:27)*

The Lord blessed this work among the poor, and it developed into quite a neighborhood commissary effort. We set up a shoe repair center by going down to the Dodge Plant for salvage belting in gunny sacks. We used the unemployed fathers of the children to sole the shoes of the neighborhood boys and girls so they could remain in school. Often when shoes were brought to us for repair, it looked as though they were asking us to put a pair of shoes on some shoelaces, but we managed somehow.

We also went out and begged for food, vegetables, soup bones, and the like. We kept people fed who otherwise would have been hungry while they waited for investigators from relief agencies to establish them on relief. One day the principal of the school called and asked if we could get some food over right away for a little girl who had fainted in class from hunger. This was a typical example of the work that was sent our way. I was a member of the Relief Council Committee in my section of the city, and the schools and other groups who had heard of our work among the poor sent many people our way for help. It was through our efforts that the city had the vision to set up more shoe repair shops to assist the needy.

We also had clothing drives: we collected, washed, and mended clothing. Shelves were filled with clean, useable apparel so we could clothe children with warm dresses, underwear, coats, hats, and mittens—everything they needed. Through this ministry to the temporal needs of the people, we were also able to minister to their spiritual needs. Many who were won for Christ during the Depression years faithfully followed the Lord. Others, of course, just as they did with Jesus, followed only for the loaves and fishes. Yet we felt that, little by little, we were entering into the ministry that God had planned for us before the foundation of the world.

* * *

A short time after my baptism in the Methodist Church, one Sunday morning our regular minister was ill. There were two men in the church who acted as local preachers, whose function it was to substitute for the pastor in case of emergency. While the congregation was waiting for the appearance of the regular minister, one of these men came down the aisle and whispered to me, "We would like to speak to you for a moment." I accompanied him to the vestibule. They told me that though they were the local preachers with the duty of substituting for the pastor in his absence, they both felt I had the message for that morning.

At this time, I had never spoken in a church in my life other than to teach a Sunday School class. I was simply petrified with fear at their suggestion. I told them I was certain they were mistaken, as I had no message and would not know the first thing about delivering a sermon before the congregation. However, they prevailed upon me to go with them to the basement to pray. They said, "Whichever one of us God will give the text to will have to do the preaching."

I Deliver My First Sermon

I did not know then even what a text would mean, but I just knelt down and prayed that somehow God would help these men take care of the service as they were expected to do. When we arose from our knees, one elder said to the other: "Have you got the text?" and he replied, "No, I haven't. Have you?" The first elder shook his head, and then both looked at me meaningfully and questioningly. I said, "I certainly don't know anything about preaching a sermon, nor do I know anything about a text, but while I was kneeling there, all that came to me was 'Whosoever will, may come and drink of the Water of Life freely.'"[4]

I did not have the remotest idea that this was a text, but they both smiled and said, "Well, you have the text." I tried to persuade them that I didn't, but they insisted. When we went back upstairs, the first elder opened the service. Then when the time came for the sermon, he announced they had a guest preacher, and that I was to bring the message. As he called me to the platform, I shook with fear and self-consciousness, but he had found the text for me in the Bible and presented me with it to read the chapter containing the text.

Strange to say, when I began to read the Word a calmness came over me I could not explain. I felt perfectly at home on the platform. God filled my mouth with the overflow of the love and burden of compassion with which He had been filling my heart since the day He saved my soul. It seemed that everyone in the church that Sunday wanted to "come and drink." It seemed that everyone wanted to partake of the Water of Life. It seemed that everyone wanted more of Him and His love. It was an experience I shall never forget and which I love to remember. The first elder said to me after the service, "We can understand why God baptized you in the Holy Spirit, for certainly He has called you to the ministry."

God's gifts and callings are without repentance, and surely we have found His callings His enablement. You will remember the covenant I had made with the Lord when I was in the hospital in Ann Arbor: that if He would permit me to go home to raise my family, I would do anything I could for Him—that I would give Him my life. So, I felt I could never say no to anything He asked me to do.

---

[4] See Rev. 22:17

A Hand On My Shoulder

It may not be on the mountain's height
Or over the stormy sea;

It may not be at the battle's front
My Lord will have need of me;

But if by a still, small voice He calls
To paths I do not know,

I'll answer, dear Lord, with my Hand in Thine:
I'll go where you want me to go.
(Hymn by Charles H. Gabriel)

Chapter 13

Stops And Steps

The reluctance and fear, the conviction of unworthiness and insufficiency, had melted away with the success of my first sermon—a sermon prompted by the faith and insistence of the elders of the little Methodist Church. The feeling that this was the right thing to do, that this was the path in which God had been leading me since I first felt *His Hand* on my shoulder, grew in me and built a sensation of confidence in the work.

The little group, which was on fire for God, was seeking green pastures and refreshing streams to satisfy the hunger and thirst of their souls. In a short while a small number of sincere Christians had begun a work in which the Full Gospel[5] was preached. This group graciously appointed me to teach the adult class. The fellowship was precious and fruitful. It was here that our commissary work among those hardest struck by the Depression was started.

It would be but natural to think that this period should have been the richest and happiest of my life. I had found my work in God and felt equal to it. I was in a fellowship of earnest Christians who had given me their trust and a position of respect. It was also about this time that our third child, Harry, was born. Another blessing from God, a more personal one, was placed in our hands for nurture and guidance to brighten and further enrich our lives. I should by all measure have been among God's happiest creatures.

---

[5] The Full Gospel: The belief that the gifts and manifestations of the Holy Spirit were not just for the historical church in the Book of Acts but are for believers today as well.

A Hand On My Shoulder

In spite of this, the darkest tunnel of my life was entered at this time. In a way, it is difficult to describe. God saw fit to hide *His Face* for a season. I seemed to be forsaken by both God and man. But I have realized in my life since then, that we all go the way of our prayers. I know now that I was running ahead of God in many directions. In my enthusiasm, in my newfound confidence and eagerness, I traveled part way down many byways that branched away from the "highroad" and wasted my effort and substance in ways out of the will of God.

It is so easy for a young and enthusiastic Christian to become swallowed up by many religious groups and practices which are not always the ways of the Lord. It is hard to keep young and eager feet straight and steadfast on the narrow path and to ignore the tempting forks in the road which seem to promise much, but which lead but to dead ends. I want to say a word of warning here to young Christians who find themselves in this position: "Stay within the shelter of the Fold, and every time you hear someone say, Lo, here is Christ, or there, go yet not after them, but try the spirit and see whether it be God."[6]

* * *

From the beginning of my pregnancy, it seemed that God cut me off from fellowship, and I surely became a "prisoner of the Lord." These were dark days, filled with sorrow and heartache, and I surely drank the dregs. There was born in my heart an understanding of the Scripture: "In sorrow and in pain shall ye bring forth your children." *(Gen. 3:16)* I had experienced the pain, but never before the sorrow of which He spoke. It was a year of virtual blackout until it seemed that the foundations of everything were crumbling. How to extricate myself from the slough of despondency, I did not know. But I realized when all else fails, when there seems no way out, there is yet a Way. So I cried out to God in my dilemma. As an answer, He spoke to me these words: "I will take your feet out of the net."

I have thanked God many times, whenever I look back over that year of darkness and suffering, that in His mercy He stopped and quieted me before Him. God has His ways of slowing us down from

---

[6] See 1 John 4:1-3

our headlong travel in the wrong direction, away from His grace. Pressure is a tool or method. And, a firm, gentle, steady pressure, sometimes scarcely felt but not to be denied, is one of God's sure methods. I am reminded in years past how the milkman, when leaving his wagon to deliver our milk, would drop a heavy weight attached to a rein on his horse, so that the animal would not stray too far away or too fast, for the pressure of the weight held him still. And so it is with us:

> Some through the waters,
> Some through the flood,
> Some through the fire,
> But all through the blood;
> Some through great sorrow,
> But God gives a song
> In the night season
> And all the day long.
> *(Hymn by George A. Young)*

I discovered the truth of His Word that declares, "I being in *the way*, the Lord led me . . ." *(Gen. 24:27)* In the depths of my confusion, pain and sorrow, God applied His firm and gentle pressure, which began to keep me still, to keep me from wandering too far or too fast from *His Way*. As always after the storm, there came a day of calm and sunshine, and of glad release as He again made me to know His love and His gentle leading.

> Out of my sorrow,
> Darkness and night,
> Jesus, I come!
> Jesus, I come!
> Into the glorious
> Light of Thy love,
> Jesus I come to Thee!
> *(Adapted from a hymn by William T. Sleeper)*

* * *

A Hand On My Shoulder

Our son, Harry, was born in 1930.[7] From the beginning of his life, he seemed to know all the answers pertaining to the fullness of God. From a very tender age, God had given him a message in song. From the time he was barely able to walk and talk, souls would find Jesus in our home as he sang to them out of his little heart. One wonders how anything so wonderful could come from such sorrow and darkness, but God works everything according to the counsel of His own will. God's ways are as far above our ways as the Heavens are above the earth.

One learns, some early, some late, not to question His ways, which are above and beyond our understanding, but to love and trust Him. The methods by which humans attempt to extricate themselves from difficulty, pain, and sorrow, which seem so logical and reasonable, are often times without result. Then, when we have exhausted our powers and know not which way to turn, God works in mysterious ways His wonders to perform.

* * *

Not immediately, but little by little, the Lord led me with gentle pressure back from the byways to the straight and broad highway to His love. The birth of my son Harry was living evidence that God meant me well and had not forgotten me. Six weeks after he was born, God gave me further knowledge of His fostering when He awakened me in the night and made me to know that He was calling my brother, Bernard, home. By all human reason and expectation, such an eventuality was not to be thought of. Bernard was only twenty-seven years of age, working in Detroit in his own business and perfectly healthy from all indications, except for a somewhat sensitive stomach. It seemed unbelievable that anything serious could be wrong with him, but I knew the Lord had spoken. Then in the morning we received an appeal to come quickly: Bernard was gravely ill. We rushed to his bedside.

---

[7] At the time this chapter was written, Harry Monville Beall was 22 years old. His mother believed that "during the year of travail, a seed was planted in his soul that would bud out to the glory of God and the help of humanity."

Bernhard had a stomach attack in the night and was in pain, but those with him and he himself had not realized the seriousness of it. So, he had delayed calling a physician until morning. When the doctor arrived and examined him, it was found that an ulcer had ruptured and peritonitis had already set in. The doctor informed us privately that after eight hours such a condition was invariably fatal.

Nevertheless, in the hope that there might be some chance, we rushed Bernard to Providence Hospital, where they opened his stomach and then closed it, having found that there was indeed no hope. During the week that ensued, he was unable to take food or water. His suffering was so intense my heart broke for him. In his pain, he completely forgot that I had a six-week-old baby and insisted on my being with him constantly.

After the year of darkness and sorrow I had been through, this seemed to be one more burden placed upon my flinching shoulders. My brother was of another faith, the one we had been raised in as children. From his own testimony, I knew that while he was a good boy and very religious, he had never yet been truly born again. Yet I felt so insufficient for the task that faced me in the short time remaining—somehow to get the Truth to him! I knew I must try, and I prayed every day and all night that God would help me to help him.

Finally came the last day—the last night. The doctor told us it was just a matter of time until the poison would reach his heart and he would be gone, but I knew the Work was not yet done. While my brother, according to his faith, clutched and prayed over a crucifix in his hand, I went to a corner of the room. There I made a covenant with God. Earnestly I beseeched the Lord that if he would cause Bernard to have the experience of being born again and would make me to know that he had, I would take my three children and strike out for Him.

God in His mercy answered my prayers and gave my brother a vision and revelation of Jesus. He died in perfect peace. Satisfied that God had heard and answered my prayer, my faith and con-fidence were restored, and I knew that these Scriptures were true:

> "I will never leave thee or forsake thee." *(Heb. 13:5)*

> . . . having loved his own which were in the world, he loved them unto the end. *(John 13:1)*

A Hand On My Shoulder

* * *

God gave me yet another evidence that He had restored me to the Way from which somehow I had strayed. One night I was called to the bedside of a woman who was dying of cancer. This was again during the years of the Great Depression. The woman's family had lost their home and had not the means for proper medical or nursing care. Nor were they even able to buy the necessary medication to relieve her pain.

In her despair and desolation, the poor woman cursed and screamed with pain. There was no repentance in her heart, but only resentment that this suffering should be visited upon her, who was as good as anyone else and did not deserve it. She had a terrible horror of the potter's field—a fear that she would be buried near a fence where people would walk over her body. In her misery and torture, practically beside herself, she raced and ranted against everything and everybody.

A friend of mine, who was this woman's neighbor, came to me one particular night through a bad snowstorm to ask me if I would go with her to where the sufferer lay. She felt I would be able to help her. No one else had been able to do so, and they were convinced that she was close to the end. When we arrived at the place where this poor woman lay, I was startled and appalled at what my eyes saw of her utter despair and helplessness. As I stood there gazing down at the ranting, raving sufferer, the Lord directed me to read a certain portion of the Scripture to the dying woman.

As I began to read, my friend told me she was amazed and taken aback for she felt that the chapter I read could have no possible bearing on the woman's situation. But it was the Lord speaking, and He used it and blessed it. The woman broke into tears and began to confess her sins. As she asked for God's mercy and forgiveness, I saw the "peace of God which passes all understanding"[8] come to her. Her testimony was: "I have such peace. I don't care now where they bury me. Even if they throw me out into the streets, I have made my peace with God and He has forgiven me."

Yet again in a short space of time, I had been given the grace to witness God going out in search of one that was lost and bringing

---

[8] See Philippians 4:7

that one home. This happening meant more to me than anyone would realize, because I knew that now I was truly out of the tunnel. God had again laid *His Hand* upon my shoulder for service.

Chapter 14

Thorborn Methodist Church

I was overjoyed to be placed upon the path again and plunged once more into the duties from which I had felt separated and confused. It was about this time that our little group, having added to its numbers and enlarged its scope, felt the need of expanded quarters. Therefore, we began the construction of a brick edifice on Seven Mile Road at Bloom Avenue, which would later be known as the North Detroit Baptist Church. My husband was out of work at this time, so he took over supervision of the parsonage.

I continued to teach the Sunday School class, rocking the handle of Harry's buggy to keep him still while I talked. We set a certain portion of the day aside for visitation in the suburbs where we lived. We put little Harry in a small wagon and away we would go every day, visiting the sick and helping people who were in distress. The study of the Word was very precious to our hearts. From time to time, God began to give us the revelation of Himself in the Word until we found it in our hearts to give everything we were, or ever hoped to be, on the altar of service to Him.

Here I labored faithfully and happily for a few years, supervising the commissary work, teaching the adult Bible class, and taking charge of a Junior Church which embraced some two hundred children. I enjoyed our work there very much, since teaching was always a joy to my heart, and the work among the poor and the training of children, a blessing and a delight.

In addition to these duties, I assisted the pastor as a church worker, as well as in the ministry of the Word. The Lord graciously allowed our work here to be most fruitful. Many souls of both children and adults were saved. Some of these children have since

Thorborn Methodist Church

graduated from the Moody Bible Institute and have gone into the field of labor for the Lord, leading others along the same happy road upon which it was once my privilege to set their own small feet. I often look back fondly upon my ministry with those precious people as a very bright and happy milestone along the long path of my walk with God. However, "God works in mysterious ways His wonders to perform,"[9] and, at this very time, He was again meeting and moving. I became aware that He was slowly and surely leading me away from this type of ministry, although into what I did not know or understand.

I was very loath to leave this group, for they seemed surely to be my people, but when the Lord is moving one has to move right with Him, whether we move hard or peaceably. It was then I discovered that God can put hornets behind you. Although He may not make you go against your will, He certainly can make you willing to go— because of the hornets, I mean.

When I held back unwillingly against His leading, distressing circumstances began to present themselves thick and fast. Had I obeyed God when He first spoke to me about leaving, I would have been saved much of the unpleasantness and the heartache that followed my act of disobedience. Finally, a day came when I had no further choice but to pull up stakes and move on. I felt like Abraham, called to go out, but where I did not know.

Note: When the little Methodist Church received a new pastor with a contrary view of the Baptism of the Holy Spirit, Myrtle and her friends were no longer welcome. So many in this congregation along with Myrtle became part of a nondenominational group who then built the small church on Seven Mile Road., which became known as the North Detroit Baptist Church. However, after a few years another minister took over the pastorate. When he learned that Myrtle had received the Baptism of the Holy Spirit and was teaching the "Full Gospel," she was removed from teaching her Bible classes and found herself without a church. (Patricia Beall Gruits)

For fully one year the Lord allowed me to sit as a woman forsaken and desolate. It seemed He permitted no one to comfort me in this lonely hour. There was even no church I could attend, no solace

---

[9] A phrase believed to have been adapted from a poem written by William Cowper based on Isa. 55:8-9

A Hand On My Shoulder

to be obtained, and why, I did not know. The friends who loved me, and whom I loved, were separated from me and I from them without any of us knowing the reason for the separation. But for the time, God caused us to be estranged from one another so His purposes in my life might be fulfilled. I was mindful of the Scripture:

> "Think not that I have come to bring peace on the earth: I came not to send peace, but a sword. For I am come to set a man at variance against his father, and the daughter against her mother, and the daughter in law against her mother in law." *(Matt. 10:34)*

It was at this time that I learned that God is a jealous God, that He will have no idols, that He wants those that are His to be separated unto Himself. He was teaching me spiritual balance according to the Scriptures:

> But the God of all grace, who hath called us unto his eternal glory by Christ Jesus, after that ye have suffered a while, make you perfect, stablish, strengthen, settle *you*. *(1 Peter 5:10)*

> A false balance is abomination to the Lord. *(Prov. 11:1)*

I did indeed suffer awhile, but gradually I became aware that the Lord was restoring spiritual balance and had indeed settled me.

Note: "I remember this time vividly. My mother would sit on the swing on the front porch, weeping—lonely and confused by the separation."
(Patricia Beall Gruits)

* * *

At last one day God caused an old friend of mine, Mrs. Woods, to be sent to me. She invited me to speak at a Ladies' Aid meeting at the Thorborn Methodist Church at Hawthorne and Seven Mile Road, of which Reverend and Mrs. William Robinson were the pastors. I remonstrated with her, telling her that because I had been saved and

Thorborn Methodist Church

had received the Baptism of the Holy Spirit according to Acts 2 and 4, I was sure I would not be welcome in this church. For much of the suffering which I had undergone in the previous church was on account of this experience of my Baptism, which was not a doctrine preached in either of these churches.

This was a matter which I could not quite understand. I did not know at that time that each church had the principle and belief of stressing certain doctrines and omitting others. Because Protestants are familiar with the Bible and encouraged to read the entire Bible, naturally I therefore supposed that everything that was in the Bible would be accepted by those who believed in reading it. I could not conceive why I was regarded as being out of order when I expressed myself as believing those things that are in the Word.

The reason for my unwillingness to speak at the Thorborn Methodist Church was that I felt I would be no more welcome in that church than I had been in the other. But my friend protested that such would not be the case. She assured me this pastor and his wife were spiritual people who loved the Lord, were unsectarian, and loved Christians everywhere, no matter what the division of their ways toward God.

Her earnestness and the things she told me lent encouragement to my heart, so I consented to go with her to the meeting. When Mrs. Woods introduced me to Rev. Robinson, I immediately felt the bond of Christian love and unity that emanated from him. However, I felt I could not betray this good man's confidence, so I asked if I could talk to him frankly and confidentially first before I addressed the ladies as I had been invited to do.

He was most gracious and kind and, encouraged by his gentleness and understanding, I related to him my experience in the Lord. He listened to the details very attentively and respectfully, and I knew that this man had a deep respect and understanding of the things of God. When I was finished my story, he was very touched. He said he felt honored that God would send such a one to his church. He assured me that he believed, even as had the Methodist minister who had first encouraged me in my early experience, that God was truly going to use me to labor in His vineyard.

After meeting with Rev. Robinson and sharing my Holy Spirit Baptism experience, I consented to speak that afternoon to the Ladies' Aid Society of the Thorborn Methodist Church. The message was blessed of the Lord. Afterward the Rev. Robinson told me he was delighted with it and the material I had given. As proof of his sincerity, he invited me to be the speaker at the Mother and Daughter Banquet to be held shortly afterward. I felt compelled to accept. At this banquet the Lord met us all most graciously. Before its conclusion, it had almost turned into a revival meeting. In fact, while we were praying with people at the altar, even babies were being dedicated. Everyone felt the approval of the Lord upon the assembly of mothers and daughters.

Rev. Robinson and his wife were most pleased with my work and the reception of it. At this time arrangements were made for me to hold Pre-Easter Revival Services at the church. This was the beginning of a long and happy association with the Robinsons, which amounted almost to a tradition, for wherever they moved in all the years following, I always arranged to give them an Easter meeting.

* * *

At the risk of interrupting my narrative, I would like to tell here of the last meeting Rev. Robinson arranged for me to hold. It was at the Methodist Church in Pontiac, Michigan. After the details for the convention had been concluded, on a Sunday afternoon prior to its opening, Rev. Robinson, who was resting in the parsonage just across from the church, was notified that the church was on fire. Before the conflagration was controlled, it had done great damage to the church interior. This shock was too much for the gentle Rev. Robinson. In a few days he had gone on to be with the Lord whom he so dearly loved. Rev. and Mrs. Robinson were never blessed with a family, and his passing was a terrible loss to her.

But in the midst of her grief at that time, she asked if I would still come for the Easter Convention, since she knew that was what her husband would have wanted. Of course I consented. For some time afterwards, while Mrs. Robinson continued pastoring, I went out to Pontiac and assisted in the Easter meetings, which were held in their basement auditorium.

* * *

Thorborn Methodist Church

To return to my story, these first Pre-Easter meetings with the fine people of the Thorborn Church were singularly blessed of the Lord. Many souls were saved and countless Christians consecrated themselves once again to the Lord. New members were also added to the church. In addition to his work at Thorborn, Rev. Robinson also pastored a little group further out called the Campbell Memorial Church. I gave this church a week of meetings during the Easter season as well.

My work with the Robinsons one night is marked especially in my memory. They asked me to speak following a children's program. As I sat on the platform during the program, I became absorbed by the thought that I was standing at the crossroads of my life—one of the turning points in my experience. So many demands seemed to me as though the drawing in various directions would be too much for me. My home was calling, my husband and children were calling, and God was calling. The call of God upon my life was as strong and poignant as was the call of my home and children, and the wish of my husband was that I should be only wife and mother. I realized that all three of these pursuits were full-time duties. How any woman who was a wife and mother could also be the complete servant of God, with a full heart of obedience to carry His message of reconciliation to a world in need, was a complete source of bewilderment to me.

As I sat on the platform that evening, it seemed for a short space of time that I was completely overwhelmed by the hopelessness of the situation I was in. All seemed to be maladjusted. Whenever I was called upon to speak God's message to others, I felt confident and strengthened. It seemed my words accomplished much toward His work in others. At the same time there was no lessening of my love and concern for my family. This indeed was a time of deep and bitter trial. I was neglecting duties, drawn this way and that. I seemed unable to give my full heart to all my responsibilities. I seemed to myself unfit. Even the clothes I was wearing were anything but what could be called presentable for platform work, so shabby were they.

When it came time for me to minister the word at this meeting, I felt indeed like an empty vessel, but presently I felt God filling me with Himself, His love, His compassion, His burden, and His wisdom. There came from my innermost being a flow such as I had never before experienced. Surely the Scripture, "for when I am weak, then am I strong," *(2 Cor. 12:10)* came alive to me. At the close of the meeting when the invitation was given, every person in the church, young and old, found a place to make an altar for their consecration unto the Lord. Many were saved, and others found again the "Bethel"[10] of their first love. Many times since that feeling of empty bewilderment, I have realized I was in God's school. I have learned that God can supply all my needs through Jesus Christ.

After the meeting, Mrs. Robinson inquired of the young people: "What was it she said that caused every one of you to go forward?" Their answer was: "We don't remember what it was that she said, but it was that certain look upon her face that made us feel the Presence of God and His call upon our hearts."

Rev. Robinson then rose up and said to the people, "I am going to prophesy that the world will hear from this woman." Everyone knew that he was speaking beyond his own knowledge, for he surely spoke as one anointed of the Lord.

* * *

After I had spent some time ministering at the Thorborn Church, one day the Rev. Robinson spoke to me about affiliating with the Methodist Church and becoming a Methodist minister. He told me he was convinced I would have a very fruitful ministry among the people that he served. I was inclined to think so too, since I had been saved and baptized in the Holy Spirit while a member of the Methodist Church. I certainly felt a debt of gratitude to these people, and I consented.

Plans were begun forthwith to take me into the Thorborn Methodist Church as a member in preparation for my acceptance as a minister of that group. I felt the seriousness of the step I was taking and gave myself up to prayer and fasting during my days at home, so that I would surely know my mind in the matter.

On the day when I was due to become a member of the church, while there in the meeting waiting to be called forth, the Lord spoke

---

[10] Bethel was the place where Jacob first encountered God for himself. When Myrtle refers to people finding the "Bethel of their first love," she means that they revisited their first meeting with God and, as a result, a rekindling of their love for Him.

Thorborn Methodist Church

to me and also to Mrs. Robinson. When she came to me to ask what I had decided to do, I told her I was feeling a very definite check from this step. Mrs. Robinson was very kind and gracious as she told me she believed I really had received the mind of the Lord in this matter.

As the days went on, all of us, including Rev. and Mrs. Robinson, were satisfied that God was leading in my life, and I should follow where I felt *His Hand* drawing me. God had other plans for me, though I knew them not yet. I was stepping very cautiously from one call of the ministry to another. Then one day, God made me to know it was at last time for me to enter upon the one ministry for which He had prepared me before the foundation of the world—the work that would be known as Bethesda Missionary Temple.

Chapter 15

My Destiny Formed

During this time of being torn between the call to do the Lord's work and the fulfillment of my responsibilities to my husband, home and family, a friend called to ask me to go house hunting with her in our neighborhood. After we had unsuccessfully scoured the entire neighborhood, we thought we would investigate the Van Dyke area by taking a short cut down Nevada Avenue, which then was a very bumpy, dirt street. The streetcars at that time made a turn just off Mt. Elliot, which was the end of the line. However, there was a little car which ran out to the city limits on Van Dyke every hour or so.

As we drove down Nevada Avenue, we noticed that the old Deaf Institute stood alone on the street except for a couple of small cottages, which had been there since this section of the city was known as Old Norris. As we drove a little farther along the street, we came past a red brick store building with flats above it on the corner of Nevada and School Avenues. As our car moved opposite this building, I felt a great presence of God come over me and an irresistible consciousness that the Lord wanted me to have that building for His work. I did not mention a word of this to my friend in the car, because down deep in my heart that was the last thing I wanted.

I loved my home, my family, and my husband, and the thought of anything else that would take me from them was most distasteful to me. Yet, I also loved the Lord and remembered the vows I had made to Him when He delivered me from my grievous illness in Ann Arbor, and when He gave me the peace that He did when He saved me. So I returned home from that ride with many conflicting thoughts and emotions racing through my heart and mind.

It is never religion, never Christianity, nor doing the will of God that rends people asunder, but the conflict that precedes the full

My Destiny Formed

surrender of one's life, heart, mind, strength, and finances to the perfect will of God for the Kingdom's sake. I pity very deeply those people who live in the constant turmoil of a call of God upon their lives without having the grace to make complete surrender. This was the place in which Jonah found himself when God called him to go to Nineveh, but instead he decided he would go to Tarshish. With that choice, "he bought a ticket and he paid the fare thereof." Anyone who goes away from the presence of God pays and pays and pays, and is overwhelmed with turmoil and regret.

Jonah, too, went through many hard places until, at last, down in the belly of the whale in the bottom of the ocean, he found himself at the end of all creatures' help and strength, knowing beyond the shadow of a doubt that no one or nothing could save him. It was there that a great revelation came to him: "Salvation is of the Lord." (Jonah 2:9)

* * *

For days after the experience of driving by this building, I went around in circles. I knew only too well "salvation is of the Lord," and I also knew the need for others to have such a revelation in this world of storm and stress. I knew many had been swallowed by terrible things and needed release, that someone had to throw them the lifeline. And I knew beyond the shadow of a doubt that that someone was me! I could not escape the conviction that sooner or later I would have to do the things which God was calling me to do, though it apparently made no sense when I considered myself, my husband, my family, and my home.

A second day my friend called, asking again that I would accompany her in her search for a home. And again I went. As we drove down Nevada Avenue once more to enter the Van Dyke district, we passed the same red brick building at Nevada and School Avenues. Again I felt the presence of God bringing me the understanding that He willed me to have that building. Still the conflict within me would not permit me to impart this knowledge to anyone, even my friend who was with me. So again I went home to more tears, more prayer, more agony of spirit.

Some short time later, my friend called again. She had not yet found a home. So once again I went out with her, along with another lady who thought she knew of a place my friend might like. As we rode down the bumpy, dirt surface of Nevada Avenue, once more I felt the presence of the Lord. As I looked out the window, I found we were again in front of the same building. By now I was becoming more confident that this was the will of God for me. However, I had at this time no aspirations or desires for the preaching ministry. I felt perhaps I could placate God by gathering up children who were not able to go to Sunday School because of the lack of transportation. I thought this building could also be used for a day of prayer and to sew for the poor. It was then that I finally told these ladies what I had been feeling concerning this building each of the times we had passed this way.

One of the ladies replied, "But how can this be? The building must surely be rented. There are curtains in the windows, and it looks occupied."

Nevertheless, I asked them to stop. We went to the door and knocked. Receiving no answer, I went around to the side entrance and met a man who was engaged in vulcanizing tires. I asked him where I might contact the people who owned the building. He informed me that the man was upstairs directing some plumbing installation and that he would call him.

The gentleman in question came down. I asked if the building was available and would he rent it for use as a Sunday School, a meeting place for prayer and sewing for the poor. He said he guessed he would. Then I told him we had no money but asked if he could hold the building for us until the first of the month. Then if I had the money for the rent, I would take it as a sign from God that we were to have the building for this purpose. Suddenly, I realized how foolish this thought must seem to a business man. So I said to him, "I am sure you think I am foolish."

He replied, "Well, if I didn't have a mother just like you in Germany, I might think you are foolish. But I understand something about these things." So he promised to hold the building unrented until the first of the month.

* * *

After the landlord told us he would hold the building, I began to wonder if I had lost my mind. We never take a step forward for God

My Destiny Formed

without wondering if we are doing the right thing. Our hearts begin to fail us for fear. We quake inwardly with anxiety and misgiving. But in those moments, an inner strength wells up within, and we know that all is well. Such was my dilemma.

Here was a mother of three small children contemplating the opening of a church. Of all my ventures, my husband and friends thought this was the most foolish. And I agreed. Why God would ever call me to such a task, I knew not. But I knew that He had called me. I could do nothing but obey. The six women who met and prayed with me every week also knew God had called me. We all agreed that we would save what we could from our grocery money every week and put it aside. When we met to pray, we would put our money together in a jar that we had chosen for a bank. If this preposterous plan of ours was truly God ordained, then we would have the required $30 at the time we needed it. If we fell far short of our goal, we would give up the idea altogether.

With this thought in mind, we all set our minds to planning economical dishes for our families. There were many meals that consisted of beans or sauerkraut or some other inexpensive dish. Daily we watched our pennies, nickels, dimes, and quarters mount up. When we met each week our money was pooled together, but because we had agreed not to count it until the end of the month, we had no idea how much money we had. When it came time to give the landlord the money or tell him that we were not interested in taking the building, we stood around the woman we had elected treasurer and held our breath as the change was counted. The amount we had saved came to $30.12. God had again proven Himself to me!

The three weeks that followed were full of activity. Because the red brick storefront building had been used to vulcanize tires, it was badly in need of cleaning. Stoutheartedly we washed the walls, scrubbed the floors, and polished the windows. It took many days of scrubbing before the building began to look like a suitable place for a church meeting.

On Saturday, June 13, 1934, three women and myself and my two oldest children went down to give everything the final touch. When we finished our polishing and dusting, we stood and looked at our clean, but empty building. We had not one chair, songbook, or piano. My heart was in my throat as I locked the door and walked home.

A Hand On My Shoulder

What I would do for the service that we scheduled for the next day, I knew not. I had no money to buy the necessary equipment. There was no one that I could turn to for aid. My dependency was in God alone.

June 14, 1934 is a day I shall never forget. It was a beautiful, warm spring day. I arose that morning full of anxiety and hope. I knew I was doing what God had told me to do, but still the problem of an empty building had haunted me all through the night. My husband, who thought I had lost all good sense and reason, looked at me and in an amused manner said, "What do you intend to do down there this afternoon?"

I replied, "Well, the floor is clean, and I am taking plenty of newspapers along with me. When they get tired of standing, they can sit on the floor." He grinned, shook his head, and walked outside.

Realizing what I had said, I hurried off to my room to pray for strength. No sooner had my knees touched the floor than a peace that passes all understanding flooded my soul. I knew that everything was going to be all right. I dressed the three children and myself nervously. After saying goodbye to my husband, we started walking toward the little red brick building a mile away. Patricia was eleven, James was nine, and Harry just three years old.

Daddy stood on the porch and watched us until we were out of sight. I could still see him in the distance, and my heart pounded. "Dear God, help me!" I cried as I hastened my pace. What the future held I knew not, but my fate was set. My destiny was formed.

Chapter 16

A Church Begins

An ever-memorable day in my life was Sunday, June 14, 1934. Here began what would be known as Bethesda Missionary Temple but was then called the Bethesda Tabernacle. As I have related, we had no money left after we had paid the first month's rent on the little red brick building. No money left for chairs, a pulpit, or a piano. No money for songbooks or for any kind of furnishings or equipment whatsoever. And, of course, there was no money for announcing the opening of the church through a single handbill or newspaper advertisement.

With my children in tow, I walked down the street toward the empty building. With fear and trepidation the thought came to me, "Who will know today is the day of opening this church, and who, if anybody, will come to this first meeting?" In my doubt and wondering, my mind went back to an experience of about a year and half before where the call of God came to me to minister the Full Gospel.[11]

Although I was ministering in a denominational church, because I had received the Gift of the Holy Spirit I knew I wasn't free to preach the Full Gospel. I knew I would have to make a change. But this step I was loath to take. I feared the fanaticism of some Full Gospel churches, the emotion-stirring demonstrations of the flesh, the noise, and travail. Drawn by the summons of the Lord, with the

---

[11] When Myrtle uses the term "Full Gospel," she means she would preach the gospel as it was in the Early Church with the Baptism of the Holy Spirit and the spiritual gifts as documented in the book of Acts. A Full Gospel Church would often be known as Pentecostal Church.

tug of my heart on the one hand and my fears on the other, the battle within me became almost more than I could endure.

I did not know what answer the perfect will of God would be for me. Could God be in all of this that seemed contradiction and confusion, that seemed to be the Spirit and yet not the Spirit of God? Was God truly in the demonstrations I had witnessed in Full Gospel churches? How could I discern the truth in this apparent paradox? And so, my dilemma faced me. I didn't want to grieve the Holy Spirit, yet I wanted to be sure that what was supposed to be God's manifestation was really so.

One day while in prayer in search of the answer to this grave problem, I was impressed by the Spirit to go to the home of a friend in Grand Rapids, Michigan. I sensed that if I could go there, and she would pray with me, I would know the perfect will of God. It was during the Depression, and my husband was not working, so I knew he could take care of the children in my absence. But transportation was the problem, as we were practically without funds at the time. Yet God, who is never too early or too late but always on time, sent a friend to me who was driving to Grand Rapids. She invited me to accompany her. Being sure God had sent her and with my husband's consent, we agreed to leave in the morning.

Upon arriving at Grand Rapids, I found my friend had a houseful of unexpected company who were relatives but not Christians. I was dismayed and wondered how we would ever have the opportunity to pray under the circumstances. However, that night we agreed we would ask God to lead the way in the morning. Again God was faithful as we were directed to Bangor, Michigan—a little town across the state. My friend from Grand Rapids drove. When we arrived at my friend's home in Bangor, we found the family all packed and ready to move! Thus, again, it seemed that the purpose for which we had come was to be thwarted, but my friend assured us there was plenty of room and time to pray.

We explained to this Christian couple the battle that was raging within my heart, and how I needed an answer from God as to His perfect plan, will, and direction for my life. They understood my predicament. In great sympathy and with supporting faith, they knelt and prayed for me while I battled for the reply down among the packing boxes.

A Church Begins

After a time, the struggle within me passed. I could say with perfect confidence and comfort, "Not my will, but Thine be done, O Lord." There a covenant was made between the Lord and me. I promised Him I would preach the Full Gospel faithfully, if He would be the Senior Partner and take care of all the demonstrations of the flesh and the spirit. As I made this covenant, peace flooded my heart. I knew God had heard me. Just before I arose from my knees, I said with a smile, "Lord, who will know I have said 'yes' to your perfect will to preach the Full Gospel?"

I was not long in learning that it is important only that God knows you have made the consecration. For upon my arrival at home in the early hours of the morning, I found a letter awaiting me. It was from the pastor of a Full Gospel mission inviting me to come and take her mission for a few weeks while she went on vacation. She stated she had prayed and asked God with whom she should leave the work, and the Lord had caused her to extend the invitation to me. She added, "Though you have had no experience in Full Gospel preaching, I think it is in the Lord's mind for you to begin."

Thus was my pilgrimage was fulfilled—a confirmation once again that when we pray in secret, God hears and rewards us openly.

* * *

It was the remembrance of this experience which came to me as I walked along the street that day toward the little red brick building. It was clean, but bare of furnishings, bare of even the minor physical needs wherewith to serve God, and with no funds to spread the word in the public print that here was a new sincere, though modest work in His name. I wondered who would know we had opened the doors —that a meeting was to begin. I wondered who would be there, and how they would know to be there.

As I recalled my pilgrimage to Grand Rapids and Bangor, and the circumstances of my struggle, and the covenant I had made with God and His immediate answer, I knew God knew. And whoever God wanted to know would be there. Upon arriving at the building, I found a number of people had already gathered for the service. To my mind it was another one of God's miracles that anyone should be present. I saw in this congregation another confirmation of the faithfulness of God.

A Hand On My Shoulder

Bethesda Tabernacle opened in 1934
Later referred to as the Mission Building

The location of the original storefront church

Chapter 17

God Had Our Address

I will never forget the picture as I stood in the doorway of what was known as the Bethesda Tabernacle that Sunday in 1934. Here in the barren little building, whose only virtue was cleanliness, stood the people who had come to the service. They were standing in groups—two and three here, two and three there. In subdued voices they were asking questions and wondering what the day would bring.

As we entered, a silence fell. I know now they were all feeling sorry for me and wondering with what mixed emotions I must have come to this service. I knew I must set an example of courage and determina-tion, and, as best I could without even chairs to sit upon, I began to arrange the group for teaching.

At this very moment, there was a commotion at the doorway. To my amazement, I found some people unloading folding chairs from the trunk of a car in front of the building. The Lord had spoken to the pastor of the United Brethren Church on St. Cyril Avenue. He had sent us a dozen-and-a-half folding chairs, not new but service-able, and a similar number of used song books, which we could have until we could acquire some of our own to replace them.

You can imagine what a feeling came over me as I saw again how God was mindful of our problems. He knew we had opened the work. He had our address, and He was still able to talk to His children. The Scripture came to my heart: "Give and it shall be given unto you; good measure, pressed down, and shaken together, and running over, shall men give to your bosom." *(Luke 6:38)*

We learn that God does not work apart from men, but He is able to employ men and all creation to bring about His will. Feeling very wealthy, we began graciously to appoint people to chairs and to supply them with the songbooks. Perhaps worn-out chairs and worn-out songbooks would not seem a token of prosperity to others, but to me, it seemed as though God had poured the wealth of Heaven into my lap. We were able to proceed with the teaching with firm confidence and the assurance that a good start had been made toward the success of the work.

* * *

God sent us very poor people in those early days. I always felt it was a mark of God's confidence and love that He would entrust to me His poor. The Scripture, "Hath not God chosen the poor of this world rich in faith" *(James 2:5)* has been proven over and over again to me. Since then the Lord has sent people of means, education, and refinement, and I have thanked Him for all of them. But there is a secret in my heart between God and me concerning the trial of my faith that was made possible by giving to me at the beginning those whom I was called upon to help and minister to, rather than those who would minister to me. For Jesus Himself "came not to be ministered unto, but to minister, and to give his life a ransom for many." *(Matt. 20:28)*

During this first service, among those who attended was a woman of another faith. This woman was an alcoholic, and her family had suffered much because of her periods of prolonged intoxication. At the close of the service she was saved and delivered, and her family who came with her was also saved.

We felt God was giving us a glimpse into the type of ministry to which He had called us. Even as Jesus was appointed "to preach the gospel to the poor; . . . to heal the brokenhearted, to preach deliverance to the captives, to set at liberty them that are bruised . . ." *(Luke 4:18)*, even so we knew too, that that was the reason God had anointed us. Our work during those early days was mainly among the destitute, the afflicted, the lost and confused, and never was work more rewarding in God's grace.

In the beginning, our thought had been merely to have a Sunday School for the neighborhood children and our own, and perhaps to have one day of the week set aside for prayer and sewing for the poor. However, the Sunday School was prolonged into a teaching and preaching service for the glory of the Lord. The blessing of His presence was so deeply felt that we were loath to leave afterwards. So very soon, we were having a morning service and evening evangelistic service. At all the meetings souls were saved, and the work was growing under the blessing and the *Hand* of the Lord.

* * *

This was during the time of the Depression, so we appointed Thursday as our day of fasting and sewing for the poor. We called our little group the "Dorcas Group."[12] We would invite neighboring women and friends to come and help us ready the garments. Those were such happy days. Our whole conversation during the time of sewing was on the wonderment of His goodness and mercy. Every garment prepared by the group was prayed over before it went out. We would ask the Lord that anyone receiving this garment would find Him as their personal Savior. It was definitely a work of faith, and it brought the results that only faith in God is able to produce. We were able to clothe and help feed many families who were feeling the pinch of those Depression days. We were able to lead many to the Lord. Many were the lost sheep brought back again into the Lord's fold.

* * *

The thought of any remuneration for the work at the church had not at this time even entered my mind, even had there been any church income to allow it. The offerings for the whole day on Sunday would average only a few dollars. With this we managed to save toward the rent for the building and the few indispensable little necessities as we went along. But I was so happy to be of service to the Lord, so thankful almost to the point of awe at the thought that God would condescend to use me in any small capacity, that the idea of compensation never even crossed my mind. As I look back to the hardships of those first years, I realize that the love and desire to serve God made what were real sacrifices seem like nothing.

---

[12]Dorcas is documented in the Book of Acts as a believer who had a heart for those in need. She sewed garments and ministered to the poor with her charity.

A Hand On My Shoulder

When finally the situation got out of hand, and I was spending virtually all my time on the work and had to have remuneration to continue, I remember well my first pay was five dollars a month. At that time, I felt almost guilty in accepting it and would not have done so had not the situation become dire.

Not having the wherewithal even for car fare, our visitations to the poor, sick, and needy took us many miles on foot in all sorts of weather. I remember how many times in the day on one of these trips, I would have to change the cardboards that I had placed in my shoes to replace the soles that were worn through or missing. However, there was no thought of feeling sorry for myself. There was such a happy urge of love that seemed to surge through me constantly. To be of service to my lovely Lord and to the needs of humanity made personal need and inconvenience seem unimportant. And I remembered constantly that God will not test us beyond what we are able, but will with temptation make a way of escape that we may be able to bear it.[13]

And, God was again about to reveal His faithfulness.

---

[13] See 1 Cor. 10:13

Chapter 18

A Ministry Of Deliverance

> "For God so loved the world, that he gave his only begotten Son, that whosoever believeth in him should not perish, but have everlasting life. *(John 3:16)*

This is the reason Jesus came, and His Father's reason for having given Him as a gift to the world. He was anointed and sent to set captives free, to open the prison houses, and to set at liberty those who are bound. None but God could think of so gracious, so necessary, a gift to give to mankind as the gift of a Deliverer. We thank God that this message of deliverance was not given to Jesus alone, but to us as well. Jesus declared,

> "These signs shall follow them that believe: In my name shall they cast out devils; they shall speak with new tongues; they shall take up serpents; and if they drink any deadly thing, it shall not hurt them; they shall lay hands on the sick, and they shall recover." *(Mark 16:17-18)*

> "Heal the sick, cleanse the lepers, raise the dead, cast out devils, freely ye have received, freely give." *(Matt. 10:8)*

Knowing that the Lord had also anointed and called me to a ministry of deliverance, I was never so happy as when the Lord would allow me to be His instrument in delivering lost and bound humanity from the clutches of the enemy of their souls. That He so

A Hand On My Shoulder

selected me was proved many times in the early days of the Bethesda Tabernacle, and through the years since those spare and trying days.

Previously I told of the deliverance of the woman who was an alcoholic—of the joy and thankfulness of her family to whom she was restored whole again. That was the beginning of a real ministry of deliverance among men and women, both young and old, who were bound by alcoholism and unable to deliver themselves without God's help. As time went on, more and more were rescued from this thrall. This work became known in all walks of life in the city, not only among individuals who had witnessed, heard, and experienced this redemption, not only among churches to whom this striving became evident, but even among those in the business community. Many of whom would send us employees who had become overwhelmed, for whom they felt sorry and had pity for their families.

The Lord was merciful through our prayers to deliver everyone who was sent to us. God's works are wonders to behold. We have seen hopeless derelicts delivered in an instant of time. We have watched as God strengthened and renewed them until once again they could take their rightful places in society as competent, dependable men and women, freed of the scourge, restored to themselves, their families, and their work.

These afflicted people all in one accord became Christians. Many of them were Spirit-filled Christians who labored and carried the burden for the deliverance of others whom they would find in life's circumstance of helplessness. Their desire was to repay God's grace by serving Him in the rescue of those who were like they themselves once were.

We even had in our congregation one brother who became the leader of what he termed "The Drunkards' Prayer Band." This group of worthy and laboring Christians, all men and women who were delivered, met once a week to pray over the requests that were sent to the Tabernacle for loved ones who were bound and helpless. It is most gratifying and edifying to receive and read letters of thanksgiving and testimony from all corners of the globe telling how these prayers were answered.

But deliverance from the hopelessness of degradation that results from chronic drunkenness was not the only weapon God gave us to wield in His behalf. We also found, going forward in faith, that the

A Ministry Of Deliverance

Lord had also given us the ministry of deliverance from addiction to nicotine and drugs. From subjection to the grip of this slavery, we have seen the possessed and the oppressed go free.

I shall never forget the joy that came to my heart when I became conscious of the fact that the Lord had also given me power over disease and sickness. We have seen infirm spirits, demons, and sickness of disease leave wrecked bodies. We have witnessed the healing virtue of the Lord Jesus Christ enter into these bodies and make them every whit whole.

We have also seen unhappy captives set free, captives as shackled and ironed as any medieval galley slave or dungeon-buried prisoners of a tyrant—prisoners of lust and unholy desire, people bound by thieving and lying spirits. From all the forces of evil, of self-indulgence, of human frailty, wickedness and weakness, it was our privilege to see the bonds struck off men and women by the incomprehensible love of God expressed through the obedient work of His ministry. We have seen the spirit of Truth take possession of life upon life in countless numbers—dedicated to the cause of Christ in a real ministry of deliverance. We have seen "mighty oaks from little acorns grow." We have learned that "little is much, with God in it." How true are the words of these two songs:

> The Lion of Judah shall break every chain
> And give us the victory again and again.
> *(Source Unknown)*

> Let the oppressed go free;
> Let the oppressed go free;
> There is deliverance in Zion for you and me,
> Let the oppressed go free.
> *(Source Unknown)*

Chapter 19

His Eye Is On The Sparrow

It pays to live in a place where God hears and answers prayer, in a place where you have confidence in God—a confidence that our God is concerned with the little things in the lives of His children as well as the greater things. He gave us a beautiful illustration when He told us that not a sparrow falls to the ground without the Father knowing it. And then He tells us we are worth more than many sparrows.[14]

I was made to realize this very surely in the early days of my ministry. We were still in the first little building that was then known as the Bethesda Tabernacle, the storefront which later was lovingly called the Mission Building. Those were lean years, years of the Depression. Money was scarce and jobs were few. As mentioned in a previous chapter, we did practically all our visitations on foot. One day a lady friend of mine, who was a good driver, and I were discussing the inconvenience and hardship of having to make all our calls on foot. My husband and I had a car, but the problem was I had never learned to drive it. Since the car was in our garage and my husband had gone out for a day's work, we decided it was time I should learn to drive. She agreed to teach me, but I was not aware that I needed a permit.

Before we started out, I laid my hand on the wheel and asked God for guidance in learning to drive. After we had been driving for some time, my friend remarked that I was making wonderful headway. She was sure I would be a good driver, when suddenly we found ourselves in an accident. Both cars were badly damaged. The

---

[14] See Matt. 10:29-31

other car was a brand new LaSalle, driven by a young boy who was crying as if his heart would break. I forgot my own troubles in trying to comfort him and told him I would be glad to go to his home with him.

When we arrived there and told the owner what had happened to the car, he was very upset and called the police. We were taken to the police station. Needless to say, my friend and I were in constant prayer, calling on God and reminding Him of His loving promises. We were bewildered and found it hard to understand why this should be allowed to happen when we had committed ourselves to Him before we started and had asked for His help.

The officer in charge asked me for my license or permit. Of course, I had to tell him I did not have either. After we had made our statements, I was allowed to return home. Since we had no insurance on the car, my husband felt very bad about the accident. We did not know what we would do to meet the expense. We were advised to get an attorney. In fact, all manner of advice was given us, but we felt no liberty to do anything but pray. Time passed. Yet we had not learned of an answer as to our course of action. We have learned that when you don't know what to do, do nothing.

Now I had been receiving letters from the other party's attorney, and all the blame of the accident was placed on me. They also mentioned the amount of money they would settle for. When I read these letters, I would spread them out before God and say to Him, "What shall I do?" One day, just when I was at the end of my resources, I went down to the Mission Building, knelt in a corner alone before God and poured my heart out to Him. I asked Him to please speak to me and tell me what to do. He answered saying, "They wondered who would roll away the stone, but when they got there they found the stone was rolled away."[15]

I was so relieved and thankful it seemed as if the weight of the world had rolled off me. God had the situation in hand. I immediately called the attorney to tell him I would be down to see him the next morning. He replied that it was about time he had heard from me. However, that night I received a telegram that my mother had passed away in Hubbell, Michigan, several hundred miles north of Detroit. There was nothing to do but to get ready and leave right

---

[15] See Mark 16:1-4.

away. But before I left, I instructed my daughter to call the attorney, explain to him why I could not keep the appointment, and tell him I would come to see him immediately upon my return.

My heart was heavy during the days that followed, realizing the tremendous loss of my mother's passing and the burden of the accident hanging over me as well. When I arrived north, I purchased a black dress, hat, gloves, and shoes for the funeral, as it was then a custom that all mourners should wear black. The very next morning after I returned to Detroit, I prepared to see the attorney. It was a very warm day in September so I reached for a light outfit to wear, when the Lord spoke to me and said, "Wear the black." I had never known before this time that God would be concerned about what one should wear. However, we learn that in certain circumstances a detail that seems of minor importance would be of major significance had one the wisdom of God.

I did not accept God's little check. Again I reached for a light, cool dress, when again I was impressed to wear the black. The weather was so warm that the thought of wearing a long sleeved black dress with velvet trim was unpleasant. So, for the third time I reached for the cooler outfit. This time the check of the Lord was so strong and unmistakable that I donned the black outfit I had worn for my mother's funeral.

When I arrived at the attorney's office, I was mentally reminding the Lord of His promise that "they wondered who would roll away the stone, but when they got there, the stone was rolled away." I found myself at the receptionist's desk asking for the attorney. Before I was able to explain who I was, I was conscious of someone standing next to me. A man's voice said, "Are you Mrs. Beall?" I replied that I was. He then said, "I thought you must be Mrs. Beall when I saw that black." I was very thankful in that moment that I had finally listened to the check of God.

The attorney was very tender and solicitous. He said he was sorry for the loss I had suffered in my mother's passing. He himself had lost his mother and realized the anguish in my heart. He went even further and said we would not have to discuss the business of the accident that day, we could arrange another time. But I told him it had been such a heavy pressure on me for so long that I would be glad to get it over with.

His Eye Is On The Sparrow

I noticed that he was very uncomfortable, almost to the point of nervousness and confusion. He opened the window as it was very warm, but the breeze blew his papers about, so he closed it and seemed very upset. I knew God was working. He finally assembled the papers again and began to read all the things I was supposed to have done in the accident. The Lord kept me very still. After the attorney had finished, he said, "Well, what do you think about it? Have you anything to say?"

I breathed up a prayer for wisdom and guidance. Then I told him that everything he had read seemed foreign to anything I had seen, heard, or experienced on the day of the accident. In fact, it left me very confused as to know what to say. Then he asked if I could pay half the money his client was asking. I replied, "No, we cannot do anything financially." Finally with disgust and relief, he tore up the papers and told me to go and forget the whole thing!

Again I knew that God had shown me that He is "a very present help in time of trouble." *(Psalm 46:1)* If we commit our way to Him, He will surely bring the things that are necessary to pass, and that no weapon formed against His people will ever prosper.[16] Truly, He is the deliverer of His people.

---

[16] See Psalm 37:5 and Isaiah 54:17

Chapter 20

An Unwitting Agent

The injustices of the world and what some of us are prone to call Fate often times leave us bewildered. Many times we wonder at the way things happen, things that seem unfair and underserved. Being human, we view these matters only from one point of view—our own. We fail to allow for or understand the Great Overall Plan which must encompass the entire universe and everyone who exists in it. However, the words of the Scripture, ". . . all things work together for good to them who love God, to them who are the called according to His purpose," *(Rom. 8:28)* have been proved true over and over again in the lives of those who are "the called."

In the course of my life, I had many proofs of God's watchfulness and faithfulness. When I would forget in the eager anxiousness of the moment's need, I would remember the countless times He had proved His all-seeing care. And many times after God had again shown Himself strong and faithful in the matter of the automobile accident, I was strengthened in faith, knowing I could trust God in all the disappointments and vicissitudes of life. I had been shown beyond doubt that I had found a friend who would never leave or forsake me but had always, and would always, be faithful. I thank God for all the hard places along the way, places that seemed to lead toward a dead end with no visible way out, because I have always found Him to be "the Way." Over and over again, I came to understand the truth of His promise that with every temptation, He makes a way of escape so we can endure it.[17]

The work of the little mission that was now called Bethesda Missionary Tabernacle grew steadily in spirituality and in numbers. It prospered, not in worldly gain, but in souls eager for God's grace and

---

[17] See 1 Cor. 10:13

in a growing knowledge of Him. He was making Himself very real and precious to all of us who were bent on doing His bidding. Those of us who had founded the work on the merest shoestring, but with the utmost confidence in His faith and help, were gratified to see there were many others who felt the need that we had—to know God in a very personal sense and to identify our daily lives with Him and His works. The lack of elaborate facilities did not deter us from offering our minds and hearts to Him with the utmost fullness and unrestricted devotion.

* * *

A missionary woman from China visited our church. She had begun her work in a strange and far-off land with no more resources than we had. She told how God had led her and her associates along the faith line, even as ourselves. She related a story of how when they had no finances to erect a building of worship, God had miraculously provided them with funds to raise up a place of worship, devotion, and study. Even though we had experienced a similar miracle ourselves, to hear of this experience on the other side of the world seemed fresh and new to me. I thought it was the most wonderful testimony of God's faithfulness I had ever heard.

At this time we had been growing in such great numbers that already our small quarters were beginning to be insufficient for our needs. The missionary's story brought to our minds again the inescapable fact that we would soon need a new and larger building to carry on the work. In the neighborhood where God had placed us, there was no available space for expansion. There wasn't even another building we could rent or buy.

Our small income, akin to the "loaves and fishes," had somehow been adequate to take care of our simple needs, and through judicious management and self-denial, we had been able to keep our bills paid. We never had anything left over that would even resemble something with which to start a building fund. Yet our need for more room was growing weekly with the addition of more members and growing activities in God's name.

Because of the missionary's testimony, faith and hope arose in my own heart, and I asked God to do something for us. As always, He heard my prayer. Sometime later, someone mentioned to me that

A Hand On My Shoulder

there was a portable church building for sale in a lumberyard on the west side of the city. Since there was no other available building in our present neighborhood, you may imagine that this news was most interesting to us.

Upon investigation, we found that this building was a little white portable church building which had been taken in trade by the lumber yard from a Lutheran congregation. They had used it as temporary quarters while they built a beautiful permanent edifice. Upon inspecting it, we found that this little white church would be ideal for our purposes.

We asked the price. I don't know what we expected, but we were thunderstruck when we were told that it would be $850. Not that this was exorbitant, but the truth was that we did not possess 850 cents. Of course, to us they might just as well been asking $850,000. It was that far removed from our resources.

Remembering that the little building which we were then occupying seemed just as impossible to come by when we first inquired the terms for its rental, I went before the Lord in prayer. I asked Him how I would go about purchasing this building without funds. I definitely felt this building was a part of us. It seemed so right, not only in size but in character, design, and in the way the news of its existence had come to us, and also in the seeming remoteness of its availability. I felt it was in God's will that we should have it.

On the first day that I prayed for this intention, I felt I had definitely gotten through to God. He put before my mind's eye a certain red-haired business man of our community. I was puzzled and confused at this, for this man was not at all sympathetic to our work. So naturally I concluded that it was not the Lord who was directing my mind to this man. Therefore, I gave up praying for that day, feeling that I must have in some way become diverted.

On the following day, I went again before the Lord in prayer and asked Him what to do. Again this red-haired business man was placed before me as the means to our need. It seemed all that long day of prayer, every time I felt I had reached God, the awareness of this man would block my praying. So reluctantly, I again gave up my devotions.

The third day, I had begun to feel a great anxiousness and apprehension of the passing of time. I knew I must soon contact God and

An Unwitting Agent

somehow receive a definite answer. The building could not be held much longer. No doubt it would soon be sold to someone else who had the ready cash available. So again, I repaired to my prayer closest. After some time, when I felt I had gotten through to God, there again was the red-haired man who was known in the community as Mr. Ed.

This time, in spite of myself and in spite of the unlikelihood of this man being receptive to our need, I began to feel it must indeed be the Lord who was showing the way—though how this could be, I could not conceive. But like Esther of old, I repeated to myself, "I will go. If I perish, I perish."[18]

So I prepared myself and went to Mr. Ed's hardware store. In a state of turmoil, I tried to formulate in my mind what I should say—how I should persuade this man who had never shown himself friendly to our work to provide the wherewithal for its growth.

When I entered his office and was ushered into his private sanctum, there were others present. Confused and embarrassed, I asked if I might speak to him privately. He seemed annoyed and replied gruffly that if I had anything to say I might as well say it then and there. This took the wind out of my sails. I was so upset that the pretty speech which I had planned fled completely from my mind. Instead of being a tactful young lady, I blurted out:

"I want to buy a tabernacle."

He looked at me blankly. Then his gaze turned absently to his shelves. Frowning in bewilderment, he turned back to me and muttered, "You want to buy what?"

I replied stoutly, concealing the despair in my heart, "I want to buy a tabernacle."

In utter dismay, he stared at me and repeated slowly, "And what in the world has that to do with me?"

Still scared stiff, but with the consciousness that this was God's errand that I was doing, I stammered, "I want you to buy it for me!"

He looked at me in complete amazement with eyes as big as saucers and said, "So…you want me to buy you a tabernacle!"

"Yes!" I replied.

---

[18] See Esther 4:16

A Hand On My Shoulder

After a long moment during which he stared at me as though I were crazy, he then asked almost absentmindedly, "Where is this tabernacle?"

"On the west side of the city."

"And how much is it?" he asked.

"$850."

There was a long pause, during which he shook his head several times, staring at me all the while as though I or he had taken leave of our senses. I was almost about to turn away when suddenly he snapped out; "Go outside and get in the car!"

Once again, I was to witness the wheels of God in operation.

* * *

As I look back over the way God had taken me, I am convinced afresh that "His callings are His enabling." Over the years at every turn, I have stopped to make sure of God's orders for my next step. When the need for expansion and extension of our modest little work into a more significant establishment first became evident, I was by no means convinced that it was really I whom God wished to lead the people further. In the back of my mind, there was always the thought, and, I am afraid I will have to confess, the hope that, having gone this far, the Lord would relieve me and permit me to be just a wife and mother as I had originally intended. The ministry, I can assure you, was not my choice. It was always with an aching and bleeding heart that I left home, husband, and children to do the will of God in public ministry. This crisis in the little congregation's affairs was neither the first time nor the last when I felt I was more wife and mother than a minister of the Lord, that my competence to do His work must be His decision, not mine.

So I asked for that decision with what was almost a challenge to God: If, as He seemed to assure me, I was to go forward in the ministry, He must provide the building and the wherewithal to carry on the work. So when this unwitting agent of the Lord bade me enter his car, and the implication was obvious that he had decided to consider helping us, I felt I had God's answer to my challenge. Something was moving inside me of praise, resignation, and exuberance as I witnessed the wheels of God's workings again on the move.

An Unwitting Agent

There was very little said between me and this stern, impassive, business man as we drove toward the lumberyard where the little church was stored. I was afraid to say the wrong thing, to disturb whatever mood had led him to this action. I fancy he could not find words to explain his behavior to himself, let alone to me.

In due time, we arrived at the lumberyard and found the little church all set up. As I looked at it, immediately my heart went out to it. It seemed everything that one could imagine and wish for in a little church situated on the outskirts of the city. It had a vestibule and even a small tower with pointed Gothic windows of colored glass. It reminded me, as I stood gazing longingly at it, of a cathedral in miniature.

Mr. Ed interrupted my reverie by asking, "Is this the building you want?"

I returned an affirmative answer. After a pause, during which he looked at me searchingly, he again asked, more firmly, "Are you sure?"

Again, I replied just as firmly as he did that I was sure. He turned and again looked at the little church for a long moment. Then he drew a deep breath and murmured, "Whom would one have to see to purchase this building?"

I replied that I presumed someone in the office of the lumberyard.

"And, how much did you say it was?"

I again repeated the figure of $850. So over to the office we went. He questioned the man responsible for the sale of the building and found it to be as I had said. He then took a check from his pocket, a check already made out and signed by someone else. He endorsed the check and handed it to the man. I wondered about this check but, of course, said nothing.

After the business deal had been concluded, the necessary papers made out and signed, we took our departure. I struggled between mixed emotions of awe, joy, and wonder. As we drove along, he finally broke the silence.

"You don't know how lucky you were that I had that check. I tried to deposit it in the bank several times, but somehow always came home with it in my pocket."

I responded, "The fact that you had that check was known. God knew you had that check."

A Hand On My Shoulder

He said, with an odd expression, "What makes you say that?"

I then told him of my experience in prayer for three days, how God kept indicating this man to me in spite of my doubt and disbelief, until I had no choice but to go to see him with my request. I saw that he was touched and amazed, and he said, "But why would God send you to me, when I am living the way I am living?"

I told him that God, who knows the end from the beginning, knows that he is going to be saved, and that God was doing something in him, through him, and for him that possibly he would understand better down the road someday. A tear stole down his cheek, and we drove some way in silence. I knew God was moving in his heart.

After a while he seemed struck by a sudden thought, and he asked me, "Where are the lots you are going to move that building to?"

For a moment I was thunderstruck. Then covered with confusion and embarrassment, I felt myself sinking right into the seat next to him. I did not reply. I could not reply. But again, he asked, "Where are the lots to which you intend moving the building?"

Finally, I found my voice: and a weak, small voice it was. I managed only to stammer, "I...I never thought of...lots!"

His cheeks slowly suffused with red, and he said, unbelievingly, "You mean to say you had me buy you this building, and you have no place to put it?"

Again I had no reply.

The man drew the car up to the curb, stopped it, and turned to look at me sternly and yet in wonder. My mind was in turmoil. What was I to say to this man? What was I to say to the congregation? And, what was I to say to God?

Finally, I took a deep breath and with a mixture of defensiveness, defiance, and faith, I said, "Well, I am a woman, and probably I don't do things the way a man would do them. But I have obeyed God's leading, and I have no money to buy lots, and don't know what I am going to do about lots. But I am sure God knows what He is going to do about lots!"

He stared at me a long moment, shook his head, and started the car again. As we pulled out into traffic, he continued to shake his head and say nothing. I was sure I had offended him and that he must think I had taken unfair advantage of him. I began to pray silently, "God help him not to be offended and for me not to say the wrong thing."

After a long while as we drove along slowly, he stopped shaking his head, and finally he muttered, "Well, you find two good lots, and I will buy them!"

I am sure that I must have been transfigured with thankfulness and joy. It was almost more than I could take. It was my turn to have a tear steal down my face. I saw again the goodness of the Lord in the land of the living.

A Hand On My Shoulder

The Portable Church and its Addition
1937

Chapter 21

The Lord Again Sends Rescue

To many people, the location where we proposed to establish our church was the most unlikely that could be imagined. When we had opened the original work, renting space in a small brick building never intended or designed for such activity, there was not too much criticism because we were fortunate enough to find room of any kind, anywhere, with our small resources. None of us dared to take a long-range view that would include concern for a permanent location.

But as the work grew and more and more people visited the little mission, nearly everyone would make the same inquiry: "Why in the world are you located way out here in the sticks? Is this the best location you could find?" When it was proposed that we not only remain here, but actually expand on the spot, the questionings, doubts, and criticism were redoubled.

Actually one could not blame them. We were within a half-mile of the Detroit city limits. And at that time, the territory all around us was unsettled—nothing but bleak commons. It was truly the end of nowhere, without bus or streetcar facilities. We were on a street that was practically deserted, except for the Deaf and Dumb Institute, which at the time was nothing but a two-story brick home and a few other small dwellings. One could hardly imagine a less reasonable place to establish a church which should demand an atmosphere of activity and some degree of population.

But we knew from the beginning our field of endeavor for God, so the answer to all questionings and ridicule was, "God knows His business." We knew that God had placed us where we were. So naturally, when our generous friend offered to purchase the lots for us, we were convinced that God had not changed His mind and must

A Hand On My Shoulder

have reserved some property for us near the old building for erection of the new.

On the day we had planned to search for property, Mr. Ed said, "I will go with you." He was very tender, sweet, and solicitous—a miraculous change from the stern, gruff, serious business man I had met that first day when God had guided my steps to his office. Just as I had hoped and expected, we found lots right next to our present location for a reasonable price, and Mr. Ed purchased two of them. Thus, with a new building, the property on which to erect it, and a congregation, it would surely seem that our immediate troubles were over, and we were on that easy road to expansion. However, we have always found there is no royal road to success.

During that very week, my husband came down with double lobar pneumonia and was almost at death's door. Instead of the normal crisis usually experienced with this illness, it went on and on. When he had lain in a state of unconsciousness for a long period of time, the doctor reluctantly told me there was no chance of his recovery, since he had an enlarged heart with fluid and pleurisy. It would be only a matter of days, as his heart was growing weaker all the time. He had wasted away to a virtual skeleton with fever.

It seems that troubles never come singly. There was no pay coming into our house, and the church was as yet unable to do anything financially for me. We had to buy oxygen by the tank for my husband's treatment, and we had completely run out of funds. Then in the midst of this dilemma, I received a telephone call from the lumberyard telling me that a large shipment of lumber was coming in that day, and they needed space for it. Our new little church would have to be moved off their property immediately. They said they could not understand the delay in moving the building, and they felt they had gone as far as they could go in storing it for us. I had previously made inquiry about the cost to transport the building across the city to our lots. The best price I had been able to get was $300 cash. I did not have 300 cents. My husband was lying at home at death's door. The building had to be moved that day. The problem seemed almost more than I could bear. So, I did what I always did when faced with a seemingly insoluble problem: I went into my bedroom and knelt down before God and prayed.

It was a very strange prayer. I said, in effect: "Lord, it is your fault that we have the building; and it is your fault that we have the lots,

The Lord Again Sends Rescue

and it is up to you what you're going to do with it from here out." I did not say this in any spirit of bitterness or resentment, but I am sure that it rose up to the ears of God as despair and desolation, for surely I was at the end of myself. In addition to all the other complications, my daughter was ready to graduate from the 8th grade and needed the things that every little girl needs when she graduates. Perhaps this was a minor matter when compared with the more important difficulties, but as a mother, it struck close to my heart and made me even more depressed. There was nothing "to do with," and the entire situation seemed more than hopeless.

After I had cried my heart out before God, Ollie, a little orphan girl who had lived with us for eleven years, came to my bedroom door and said, "Mother, there are two gentlemen at the door to see you."

I shook my head and replied, "Ollie, you will have to take care of them yourself for my eyes are all swollen, my nose is red, and I am in no condition to receive anyone just now."

She left, and in a few minutes returned and said, "I got rid of one of them, but the other insists upon seeing you."

So, I dried my eyes and came out, very embarrassed, to meet a man I could not remember ever having seen in my life.

He said, "I beg your pardon, but I was in prayer this morning. God made me to know you are in need of some money, so I brought it to you, and here it is."

And with that, he laid in my hands six fifty-dollar bills. I was thunderstruck and awed. Though my prayers to God in all sorts of difficult situations had always been answered, never before had they been answered so promptly or so directly. When I saw the hand of God, a perfect confirmation of that which He had called me to do, I was strengthened in heart, in mind, and in purpose, to go all the way my Savior would lead me.

I thanked the gentleman as best I could, but words were too little for the great help he had given us through God's direction. I don't think he fully realized what a messenger and angel of mercy he was in the hands of God. Before he left, he told me he had been healed of arthritis and tuberculosis while just sitting in a meeting in our church. He said he felt so honored that God used him to help one of His servants.

A Hand On My Shoulder

I lost no time in calling the lumberyard to order the building moved. So it was that almost overnight our neighbors saw the church grow up like a mushroom. The expansion work that was the Bethesda Missionary Tabernacle was on its way to becoming the Bethesda Missionary Temple—the great armory of God in this manufacturing city of Detroit.

God again had sent rescue in time of disaster. We all felt strengthened, refreshed, and resolute in the happy task of performing His work.

Chapter 22

Miracles In My Own House

Our little white church was erected almost overnight. Since it was a portable, pre-fabricated building, the task of raising it was a comparatively simple one. So it was that our neighbors returning home from work in the evening saw a church standing in the path through the field they had crossed that morning on their way to work.

As soon as the little building was ready, and the seats which God made it possible for us to have were installed, we moved from the Mission Building[19] across School Street to our new church, which would be called Bethesda Missionary Temple. The new church seated 250 people, and the blessing of the Lord was very much in evidence during the dedication service that first Sunday. From that day His presence never left us; it only increased as the days went on.

* * *

While God was answering my prayer regarding our new church building, things at home were getting worse. My husband's condition did not improve. The weather was cold. We were running out of fuel without the means to renew our supply. We lived in a frame house which was not too well constructed. Without proper heating, it seemed the cold winds reached through to us freely and easily. I had prepared Harry for the day, as he was still in a coma at this time. Then I readied myself for some visitation of other sick folks of the congregation. Just before I left, I gave Ollie strict orders not to use

---

[19] Formally called Bethesda Tabernacle or Bethesda Missionary Tabernacle

the last chunk of coal which was in our coal bin while I was away. I instructed her to put on a sweater if the house got cold, for we needed to save that last bit of fuel to use during the night as we took care of my husband. She promised she would not touch the coal, and I went about my pastoral duties.

When I returned to the house a few hours later, to my surprise and disappointment smoke was pouring from the chimney and the house suffused with warmth. My heart sank within me as I concluded that Ollie, in her girlish way, could not have understood the importance of my instructions. As I entered the house, she must have seen by my expression that I was very displeased by her disobedience. She hastened to reassure me that she had not forgotten my instructions but that God had performed a miracle. She led me downstairs to the basement and showed me a bin filled with coal. Then she told me the following story.

It seems that one of the members of the church had come to the door to inquire after Mr. Beall's condition. Upon being told that there was no change and casting about for some helpful service he could perform, he asked if there were not some ashes in the basement he could carry out for us. Ollie thankfully replied that there was a tub of ashes too heavy for us to manage. He went down into the basement. There before him was our empty coal bin—empty, that is, but for one lump of coal lying in the center of the floor reserved for the long, chilly night ahead. At the sight, immediately there came to his remembrance a dream he had had the preceding night, wherein he had seemed to enter a basement and saw the coal bin open with one lump of coal upon the floor. In his dream he heard a voice telling him to fill that coal bin, and he had done so. Upon seeing our empty coal bin, he realized immediately the Lord had spoken to him in that dream. Consequently, he went out and ordered coal to be sent to the house at once.

We have always found the Lord to be an ever-present help in time of trouble. We have learned through Him and know that, for us at least, it is far easier to trust God than man. We have also proved that the invisible things are more truly real than the things that are visible—for the things that are seen are temporal, while the unseen things are eternal.

Miracles In My Own House

As we learn to press our claims on the promises of God, finding that they are true and faithfully fulfilled, we also learn that God has claims that He can press upon us. When Mr. Beall was very low and unable to be moved to the hospital because of the condition of his heart, we had to buy tanks of oxygen for him. There was no income, and what little money we had was fast running out. Finally the day came when another tank of oxygen was needed. We were completely without funds. I went before the Lord in prayer, beseeching again for His mercy. The Lord spoke to me and said, "I have given him free air for fifty years, and he has never even given Me the tithes that belong to Me."

I pleaded with the Lord and told Him that it was through ignorance and unbelief, not having the proper training, that this omission was caused. I promised God that if He would again show mercy and supply our need, and if my husband lived, he would never again be found guilty of "robbing God." My husband and I were taught a lesson that we pray we will never forget: one-tenth of all we possess belongs to God, and we are to bring that tithe and offerings into His "storehouse"[20]—the church where we receive spiritual food. And God will also reward us for good or bad, according to our faithfulness with the remaining nine-tenths.

* * *

God supplied coal and oxygen, but the pneumonia my husband had contracted had weakened his heart to the point that the doctor who had been treating Harry came to me.

"Mrs. Beall," he said, "your husband cannot live beyond another half hour, and if you have not gotten in touch with his relatives, I would advise that you do it now. Why don't you go into the other room now and use the telephone to call your people and his?"

I realize now he wanted to spare me the heartache of seeing my husband pass on. I went into the room where the telephone was, not to do any telephoning but to face God. I stood there in the room for a moment after I had closed the door, and I prayed:

---

[20] See Mal. 3:8-10

A Hand On My Shoulder

"Well, Lord, now it's just You and me. I read in the Word that 'His salvation was for thee and thy house,'[21] and I have believed it with all my heart and soul, beyond the peradventure of a doubt. And because I so loved my husband and my children, I was willing to suffer anything in order to be obedient to the call of God on my life—knowing that no price was too great to pay for the salvation of those I dearly loved. I left my husband and children days and nights, in all kinds of weather to do Your work. Many times I have walked backward watching the lights of my home as far as I could see, weeping with intense longing to be with my family, knowing that I had hurt my husband by leaving him. But I felt it was because of my love for him that I must keep close to You, because I was positive he would be saved. And, now, Lord, the doctor says he will be dead in a half hour, and he is not saved. If this promise of 'salvation for thy house' is a lie, then the whole Book is a lie, and I have been a fool to break up the happiness and fellowship in my home for something that isn't true. If he dies without You, then I have been a fool."

As I came out of the room, my children had just arrived home from school. I took them to the basement where I laid out newspapers on the basement floor next to the furnace, and we knelt down to pray. Being deeply ashamed of having approached God with such a spirit of complaint, I asked for His forgiveness, for His mercy, and for a miracle of healing. As we wept before the Lord, God who is always a loving Father, spoke to my heart: "This sickness is not unto death, but for the glory of God, that the Son of God should be glorified..." *(John 11:4)*

With great relief and thankfulness, I answered, "Thank you, Lord, that is all I wanted to know."

---

[21] See Acts 16:31

I turned to my children and declared, "Your dad is not going to die."[22] As I returned to my husband's bedroom, I was asked, "Did you contact his relatives?"

"No. I did not call any of them."

"You had better do it right away. Your husband has only a few more moments."

I replied, "No, doctor, he is not going to die."

The doctor looked at me carefully and in silence for a moment. Then he said I had better go and lie down for a while. He then asked the nurse to take me into my room to rest. I know he must have thought I was beside myself.

But I said, "No, doctor, I know what you are thinking, but I have just heard from God, and my husband is not going to die."

He shook his head and said, "I'm sorry, but he is all but dead already." Then, curiously, he went on, "What did the Lord say?"

After I told him, he again shook his head and again insisted, "I wish it were so, but your husband is finished."

But again I declared, "No, he is not.

Seeing it was useless to try to persuade me, the doctor said no more, but simply stayed, waiting in silence for some time after that. Yet my husband did not die. Not understanding what it was all about, the doctor finally left, advising me to telephone him when my husband had passed.

When morning came, Harry was still alive. So the doctor decided he would take the chance of moving him to the hospital—a step he had feared to take before because he was afraid the moving would cause the patient's heart to stop. The doctor went out to make the arrangements.

While the doctor was gone, a friend of mine and I were in the room just outside my husband's bedroom. Suddenly I heard him call my name. This was the first time he had spoken in all those days. I rushed into his room and found him looking so pitiful and emaciated from the terrible fever, but he was awake and rational.

---

[22] As Patricia Beall Gruits and her brothers were praying with their mother for their dad to be healed, she distinctly remembers how when the word of the Lord came to her mother, there was visible change in her countenance. "Whenever she said she heard from God, we knew she had and it would come to pass."

A Hand On My Shoulder

He said to me, "If you could pray for me, the Lord would heal me." I was astounded, for prior to this time because of his resentment of my activities in the Gospel, he had refused prayer completely.

I said to him, "Are you willing to confess yourself a lost sinner and to ask for forgiveness?"

"Yes, I am." And so complete was his surrender to God that he said, "I am even willing to be what they call a 'Holy Roller' if necessary!"

We immediately began to pray for him, my friend and I, and God performed a miracle. He raised my husband up to his knees on the bed—an impossible thing for a person to do naturally who had not been able to lift even his head for weeks. Harry said that Jesus came to the foot of his bed and offered him His hand, and it was Jesus who raised him up. Then from the kneeling position, he was raised to his feet—feet that looked like spindles. Not only did he stand upright in the bed, but he began to jump up and down like a child, dancing on the bed, praising God while he bounced up and down on the springs!

My friend and I were so stunned, yet so filled with rejoicing, that we scarcely knew what to do. Then Harry asked for his slippers and robe. He walked into the living room and was sitting in the chair when the doctor returned.

When the doctor saw him, looking like a skeleton sitting in the corner of the chair, he cried, "What in the world is going on here?"

Harry replied, "I'm healed!"

If you can imagine a skeleton speaking and declaring he was healed, you can conceive of the doctor's reaction. He took out his stethoscope, testing Harry's heart and back, and then said, "By George, the air is going through the lungs!"

This doctor was our old family physician, a man dearly beloved by all who knew him. He was of another faith, but he loved God. He went out and called the neighbors to come in and see a modern-day miracle. He told them, "It is nothing I have done or could do to help this man. This is surely God."

We know that "God works in mysterious ways His wonders to perform."[23] God was leaving a testimony in our neighborhood and to

---

[23] A phrase believed to have been adapted from a poem written by William Cowper based on Isa. 55:8-9

all of us that He is still a miracle-working God. He is a God who keeps His promises. He is always faithful!

* * *

After my husband's miraculous healing, he gained strength daily, and the determination and consecration of his heart was fortified as well. True to his promise, when at death's door he had asked me to pray for him as a confessed sinner, he proposed through his healing that he, too, would give his life to the work of the Lord, although at that time, he did not know in what capacity he would be called.

Yet this knowledge was not long in coming. We remember that when Solomon was called by the Lord to erect the Temple, in His omniscience God gave each worker wisdom for his part in the construction: wisdom to the carpenters, wisdom to the hewers of stone, and so to each artificer for his share in the task. And so it was with my husband. God gave to him knowledge and wisdom in building and in the arts of maintenance required to keep all things in good running order for the comfort and facility of the parishioners and children in the church and Sunday School. May I add here that, without his labor of building, maintenance, and care, we could never have been enabled to do what God called us to do. We thank God for my husband's ministry of love, for he is as one of God's hidden ones.

So many times we are wont to think of the ministry in terms of a leader speaking from a platform, being seen and heard, and receiving the reverence and applause of the congregation, but there are many workers in the Lord who render services of equal value out of everyone's sight but God's. Yet these are indispensable. Of such are the builders and architects of God's Temple and such is true in the case of Harry's ministry. He is unseen, but it is because of his willingness not to be seen and yet to labor that we have the comforts in the Temple and all of its adjoining buildings.[24]

---

[24] At the time of this writing, Easter Sunday 1954, the church consisted of four large buildings to accommodate its growing work. Sunday School attendance was just over 2,000.

Chapter 23

Spoken By God Through His Prophetess

We had occupied our new little white church for about a year when we found that because of God's "adding-to," our space was again filled to overflowing. I have ever been conscious from the first day of my ministry that it was God who gives the increase, so we asked God what to do. In prayer one day, He led me to envision a new wing on the building. After I had prayed, I told the prayer group what God had shown me and how conveniently it could be done, provided we could find funds to defray the cost. To my surprise, one of the women in the group stood up and simply said, "You put the wing on, and I'll pay for it."

So work began immediately on the plans. When the erection of the new wing was completed, we had space for an additional hundred persons. Yet it was not long before I saw this space rapidly filling up because of God's continued increase. I foresaw that in a short time the problem of facilities would again be facing us. When I again went before the Lord and asked Him what His orders were for the future, the Lord showed me what He wanted. He told me to "build an armory." I was stunned. Ministers expect to be told to build a church, or a tabernacle, or a temple, but why should God instruct a minister to build an armory? I was in great confusion of mind. Again I called upon God to ask Him what He meant by an armory. He replied, "A place where soldiers get equipment." Well, that sounded good, but I still could not conceive what sort of place He meant. I asked "How large a place, Lord?" and the answer came back, "To seat 3,000 people."

It was too much for me. I was filled with fear and consternation, for I was sure it could not have been God who spoke these strange things to me. So I waited for a while and then went before God again. I pleaded with Him until I could again hear *His Voice*. But He was merciful and assured me with an assurance which I never again lost. It was He who was speaking; it was to be an armory, and it was to seat 3,000 people.

Yet I was afraid and ashamed to tell anyone what God had told me. I felt if I repeated it, it would sound like conceit, ambition, or the ranting of a mad person. So for the time being, I hugged the secret to my heart. I resolved to continue to pray until I should unmistakably hear the *Voice of the Lord* say to me, "Rise up and build!"

* * *

During this time, God gave me a vision. It seemed as though I were walking alone in a dry and parched country, carrying a small wooden bucket which was filled with water. Suddenly I became aware that there was a terrible drought upon the land in which I was. I realized the great preciousness of the water I was carrying, and the importance of careful guardianship of the little bucket and its scarce contents. As I walked along slowly and cautiously, contemplating the great responsibility that was mine as the custodian of this small but precious burden, I became aware of a deep rumbling somewhere in the distance ahead of me—a sound as of distant thunder. I stopped and lifted my eyes to discern the source of the noise and saw what seemed to be a great cloud of dust approaching me.

As I watched, there gradually emerged to my view a tremendous herd of cattle, thundering toward me at great speed. It came to me that these cattle were conscious of the water in the little bucket I was carrying. They were stampeding in a mad rush to gain possession of it. Terrified, I breathe up a prayer to God, saying, "Lord, what shall I do? These cattle evidently know I have this water, and though there isn't enough for even one of them, they will kill me in an effort to obtain it."

An answer was returned to me: "Wait until they reach where you are standing, then leap to one side and let them pass." I followed these instructions. When the cattle had sped by, carried forward by their own momentum and the headlong pressure of their fellows, I realized immediately that in my carefulness I had not spilled a single drop of the precious water in the bucket. This gave me great joy, because I was aware that this water was very scarce and priceless.

As I stood there, thanking the Lord for my deliverance and that of my valuable charge, I heard another great noise similar to the first. I looked up to see another herd of cattle stampeding toward me from a direction opposite to that from which the first had come. These cattle were like the first in appearance. They were red, sleek and shiny, seemingly fat and well-fed. But it was obvious that they were shuddering from great thirst, for their eyes were staring wildly and their tongues were hanging out of their mouths. They, too, seemed to have knowledge of the water I carried and were bent upon taking it from me. Again I cried out in fear, for I knew not what to do. Again the same voice replied: "Jump over where you were the first time to the other side."

I obeyed the instructions. Again the herd of cattle swept harmlessly past me. I was made aware for a second time that I had succeeded in saving the water that had been entrusted to me without spilling a drop. Then for yet a third time, I heard the now-familiar rumbling in the distance. As I lifted up my eyes, I saw still another stampeding herd of cattle coming toward me—just like those in the first and second instances. They were well-fed and sleek, but with their tongues hanging out of their mouths, wanting the water I was carrying. It was an awful sight. Yet in spite of my horror, my heart ached for the terrible thirst these poor cattle were suffering. But I knew the little bucketful of water would not have quenched the thirst of even one of these great beasts.

So I cried out in supplication. Again the voice answered, this time saying, "Look over the precipice." I had not been aware that my last leap had carried me to the brink of a high precipice. With great trepidation and a fear of the awful height, I looked over the edge. Far, far below, at a depth to which I could barely see, flowed a wide and wonderful river of crystal-clear water. It was flowing rapidly, dashing itself against the walls of rock and breaking up into spray that resembled diamonds in the brilliant sunlight. So tumultuous, cold, and clear seemed this blessed stream, so plentiful its cascading billows, that I said to myself in great yearning, "Oh, if I could only reach that river, there will be more than enough water for all these thirsty cattle."

In spite of the precipitous nature of the banks above the river, I determined to try to reach it. So I started down, slipping and sliding and all but tumbling down the steep embankment. As I did so, I heard a great commotion on either side of me. I then became aware that the herds of cattle were sliding down with me. We all reached the river together.

In my eagerness, I felt a wonder as to the source of this flowing water. I raised my head to look up and beyond toward the distance from which the current flowed. Far away in the distance I saw "El Shaddai"—"The Breasted One," (the Lord)—whose supply is enough. The water flowed from His breast.

Then I saw the cattle drink and drink and become at last satisfied and refreshed. As I saw them go away, no longer parched and thirsty, I realized they, too, had become "Breasted Ones" and would go forth to satisfy the thirst of the people.

This was the end of the vision. After it, I was sure that God some way somehow would allow us to discover a river (a spiritual river) that would bring satisfaction and feed the hungry until they, too, would be able to go forth and feed others. And, indeed, the day did come when people came from all the corners of the earth to the "river" at Bethesda. They were satisfied and went away convinced that they, too, had something to give—bread for the hungry and drink for the thirsty.

* * *

Another confirmation to build the armory came one evening in a prayer meeting. One of our deacons stood up and shared a night vision he was sure was from the Lord. He had seen a huge brick structure on the corner of our property. In trying to convey the great size of the building, he went on to relate how he saw cars parked for many blocks in all directions surrounding the tremendous structure. He was most insistent in trying to impress us strongly that God had given him a vision, but his efforts were unnecessary because everyone knew that it was a visitation from the Lord. I, above everyone else, was aware that God was merely confirming to my heart once again the call to build an armory.

***

A Hand On My Shoulder

At this time we still had not received the outpouring of the Holy Spirit upon our people. There were only a few of us who had been baptized with the Holy Spirit. We had been praying for a long time that God would send an outpouring beyond what we were experiencing, for we were constantly receiving blessings from the Lord in souls being saved, bodies healed, and a continual increase in numbers. Yet the Holy Spirit was not fully manifested unto us.

Finally, God heard our prayers and caused Brother and Sister Alvin Branch to be sent to us with a special ministry. They had a house trailer which they parked in a vacant lot next to the church. They said God had definitely sent them. It was unfortunate that at this very time a very famous evangelist of the hour, Jerry Owen, was holding meetings at the Berea Tabernacle in Detroit. His ministry was very spectacular; he claimed to see Scriptures written on the walls. People came from far and near to see and hear this strange phenomenon.

It surely looked as if Brother and Sister Branch had come to the city at the wrong time, but God's ways are not our ways. They were confident God had sent them to accomplish a mission. The Branches showed a very kind and lovely spirit by encouraging everyone who wished to hear Jerry Owen to go and attend his meetings. But for those who wanted to stay, they would be happy to minister to them.

God mightily blessed their stay with us. Their ministry was so rich, and the saints were built up and strengthened from the Word of God. The last day of their stay with us will always be an outstanding day in my memory. In that last service, Sister Branch stood up and prophesied. I had never heard prophecy before. What she said gripped my heart with such a confirmation that it has had a settling and establishing force in my life. As she stood there, she prophesied what she was seeing in her vision. She prophesied the Armory into existence. She spoke of a huge brick structure which she could see on the corner of the property, and she told of its size. She told of the multitudes that would be coming and going, being blessed of God. She prophesied that God was sending the greatest revival of all history to this place. As a sign that all this would come to pass, she prophesied, "As we leave here, God is going to pour out His Spirit, and people will be baptized in the Holy Spirit."

That night, one young lady received the Baptism. This was the first Baptism we had had in the church, but within ten days, sixty

Spoken By God Through His Prophetess

more were baptized in the Holy Spirit.[25] It was a common occurrence to come to the church in the morning and see the people slain under the power of God, receiving the glorious Baptism in the Holy Spirit. We heard children speaking in other tongues, down between the seats, glorifying God. From that day to this, God has never withheld this outpouring.

Soon, with the coming into existence of the Armory, all that was prophesied would be realized. God said, "In the beginning was the Word, and the Word was with God and the Word was God . . . and without Him was not anything made that was made." *(John 1:1,3)* God spoke everything into existence, and I feel confident that the Armory of Bethesda Missionary Temple became a reality because it was spoken by God out of the mouth of His prophetess.

---

[25] It was during this time that her daughter, Patricia Beall Gruits, at the age of 14 received the Baptism of the Holy Spirit.

Chapter 24

The Beginning Of The Armory

As soon as the wing to our little white church was completed and furnished, we felt we were well accommodated for some time to come and could turn our hands and hearts fully to the spiritual works of God's grace. But almost before the paint had dried on the new wing, it was filled to overflowing with those hungering for the Word. Again we were faced with the problem of building to receive the endless stream of believers. It seemed to us then that our whole ministry was destined to be spent in finding ways to make further room to accommodate God's increase.

God had given us orders to "build an Armory that would seat 3,000 people." He had also given us the plan and pattern of the building in directions so clear and unmistakable, we find it strange to remember that we could have had any doubts or trepidation in following His guidance. It was also evident that at our rate of growth with the constant increase of our numbers, which showed no signs of diminishing, the need for the 3,000 seats which God had demanded we provide would be reached before too long. Yet, when we actually met as a committee to carry out what we felt definitely was the plan of God, because of the fear of so tremendous an undertaking, we found ourselves making plans to allow for our lack of faith in God's magnificent provision.

In the pattern which He had given us for the Armory, there was no representation of a full basement. But when we began to reason among ourselves with earthly logic, it seemed we could not visualize a building without a basement. Therefore, we proceeded to make plans to build a basement church first, promising ourselves that we would fulfill God's greater plan after we had defrayed the cost of the

The Beginning Of The Armory

basement structure. (I may say here that God showed His disapproval of our lack of faith and courage by permitting us to sit in this basement for several years.)

* * *

We made arrangements to have the little white church and its recently added wing raised up on rollers and moved a few lots away. The work of excavation for the basement church began. It was a huge undertaking. As the great steam shovel moved in and began to tear up the earth, the hole in the ground seemed monstrous. The whole undertaking was so beyond us that I was almost ashamed for anyone to know of my connection with it. As the structure began to take shape, it seemed to me one of the largest of its kind I had ever seen. Now, I thought in a feeling approaching panic, we shall go from the embarrassment of poverty in accommodations to an embarrassment of riches in unneeded, unused space. I wondered, too, where the money would come from to pay the cost of this huge structure.

But God provided. The day finally came when the basement building was completed. We were ready for the opening and dedication service.[26] On the day before the service, I looked over the auditorium with seats for approximately a thousand persons. I wondered where in the world the people would come from to fill it. However, when the service started every seat was taken. There were people standing against the walls on three sides as well! It was a great miracle and a great service. God's presence was there to bless. From that day on, God continued to bless us until incredibly we would soon find ourselves yet again without room and facilities to accommodate the increase God continued to bring. But more on that that later.

* * *

While we used the new quarters, the Basement Church, for the greater Glory of God and the continuation of His work, we were told

---

[26] The Basement Church was completed in 1939 at a cost of $11,900. The architect was P.J. Funke.

A Hand On My Shoulder

time and again by visiting missionaries who had traveled from coast to coast that Bethesda was an oasis in a desert. In truth it surely was. People were saved in every service. People were receiving the Baptism of the Holy Spirit constantly. Miracles of healing were performed repeatedly, and the good report of God's blessing was spread throughout the land.

Prayer groups met every day and prayed for hours. They prayed for the boys at war[27] and for those who were saved during our church meetings—people from all walks of life and every religious belief. Homes were united. Reconciliations were made between husbands and wives, between parents and children. Alcoholics were delivered. Drug addicts and other victims received complete rescue.

* * *

Note: At the beginning of World War II, God gave my mother a word: "pray on the radio." Thinking that these were lyrics, she inquired of family and friends if they knew of any song with this phrase. Soon after, she was contacted by WWJ, a major radio station in Detroit, to pray on the radio at noon for America and our servicemen – just as pastors throughout the Detroit were also being asked to do. A short time later after she had prayed on WWJ, another radio station, WJLB, offered her a 30 minute daily morning program. When this radio time was offered, she knew it was the fulfillment of the word God had given her to "pray on the radio."

In 1943, she began to broadcast "America To Your Knees" from the platform of the Basement Church. For every broadcast, she sought God for a fresh "word" that would touch the hearts of the people. I supported Mother by playing the organ. Following every broadcast, there was a time of prayer. Parents and friends of servicemen flocked to this prayer meeting, weeping before God for the safety of their children and friends—and that God would bless America and restore peace. God was faithful because not one of Bethesda's servicemen was lost during World War II. (Patricia Beall Gruits)

* * *

Following the War, God spoke to us again: "Rise up and begin the work of building the Armory!" This time we believed God. We

---

[27] World War II

The Beginning Of The Armory

would build an armory according to God's plan. With renewed and swelling faith, we believed that every brick, every ounce of concrete, every stick of wood, the hardware, the steel, the labor, and even the seats for it were already prayed in! Though there was nothing in evidence either of money or material to begin the great work, we had every confidence and assurance that as we went along, the mighty *Hand of God* would go along with us.

But that confidence was soon tested. To build, we needed a permit. Since the time we had built the Basement Church, our neighborhood had been rezoned into a strictly residential community. Therefore, it became necessary to petition the Zoning Board for a hearing to secure a permit to build. Many of our neighbors, being of a different faith, were not in sympathy with what we were trying to achieve. On the day appointed by the Zoning Board for our hearing, these people were notified to be present to state their case in opposition to our request for a permit to build a Temple that would seat 3,000 people. A goodly number were in attendance to protest our petition to be excluded from the provisions of the residential zoning ordinance.

The Chairman of the Board asked these people to state the reasons for their opposition. He questioned each in turn. It became apparent that the whole reason for their not wanting this new church established in their community was that they felt they had stood all they could from us in our present building. Of course, this generalization was not sufficient grounds on which to base a judgment, so the Chairman persisted in his questioning in an effort to ascertain the particulars. Eventually the objections resolved themselves into one principal complaint: it was because of our constant praying. The dissenters informed the Chairman that they heard our people praying as early as 4:30 in the morning when some of them were leaving for work, and we were still praying when they returned from work at night.

This praying, they complained, would then continue throughout the evening. They said they knew people remained in the church and prayed constantly until 1:30 or 2:00 o'clock in the morning, when they finally saw the lights put out in the building. Then, they stated, the whole process would begin all over again at 4:30 that same morning. The Chairman was incredulous. He said to them, "You surely do not expect me to believe that in this day and age, in a city the size of Detroit, that there are people praying almost constantly as you say." But each one assured him with vehemence that at all hours of the day and night, whenever they passed our church, they could hear our people praying through the open windows.

The Chairman, finding this hard to believe, questioned them again very searchingly and painstakingly. He was unable to shake their declaration that this was not only true but often even worse than they had said; frequently the praying was actually on a 24-hour basis, entirely around the clock without cessation. Finally convinced, the Chairman thought silently for a time and consulted his colleagues on the Board. Then he declared he certainly would be in favor of granting our petition to build, for he believed that the city of Detroit was in need of a church where the people still prayed in this manner.

And so we were granted our permit, and the great work was ready to proceed. The patience, faithfulness, and unremitting power of the prayer groups surmounted what seemed like an insuperable obstacle. The irresistible power of prayer was once again demonstrated; the faithfulness of our people justified. Though their prayers which had puzzled and disturbed our neighbors were not directed at the results of this hearing, but rather were concerned with the objectives of healing and rescue, they were, however, an indirect reflection of our faith in erecting the Armory for the glory of God and the ultimate reconciling of all opposition.

Repeatedly during the days of building the Armory—a monumental task beset with difficulties and trials— regardless of the obstacle that presented itself, we never had any fear that what God had directed us to do would be accomplished. We knew without doubt that God had given the orders to "rise and build." Therefore it was already as good as done. We thanked God again and again for the blessed assurance that He who had begun the good work was also able to finish it.

The Beginning Of The Armory

Bethesda Missionary Tabernacle,
also called the Basement Church
1939

Chapter 25

The Temple Rises: 1948

In receiving the Lord's orders to erect the Armory, which was also referred to as the Temple, I seemed to envision while in prayer the design of the finished building. When the architect was called, I described the plan I felt God had given me. After he had drawn it up according to scale, he remarked: "Well, you certainly got the plans somewhere, for they are really workable." I think I am able to understand the feeling Noah must have had when he saw before his eyes the plan God had given him for the Ark, because we know that anything that is God-given is always workable.

Finally the building got underway. The great steam shovels and all the other necessary equipment for the huge excavation were on the job. The laborers with complete confidence were putting in their hours of labor. Watching them work, I realized what all of this meant to the livelihood of many families. Many times this thought brought a sinking of my heart as I reflected that I had no visible finances. All I had was my faith in God that when their work was done, we would have the necessary funds to pay them since they were working in good faith, believing we were financially able to pay them.

But I have this to say for the glory of God. There was never a part of the work completed, never a bill handed in, that God did not prove Himself faithful. By means and methods known only to Him, He enabled us to pay every bill promptly when it was due. And I might add, the bills for so large a structure were not in the hundreds of dollars, but in thousands. We had bills turned in for $14,000 and $20,000. Our seats alone cost $45,000 and the steel $75,000.[28]

---

[28] The $75,000 bill in 1948 would be about 1.1 million dollars today.

The Temple Rises: 1948

One such bill was turned in by a contractor who had heard we were building on faith. Evidently he had no faith in our faith, for he handed in his bill with rather a hard spirit, saying he must have his money by the next morning. It happened that I had no money at all, not a cent to meet this particular bill, because I did not expect it would be presented so soon. We had a small gathering that evening for prayer. I told the people that, though I had no money, I had to have several thousand dollars by the next morning. A gasp went up from the gathering. When I heard it, I said: "Why do you gasp? God owns everything, and God will provide."

Then I saw before my very eyes our lovely Lord pouring out upon His people the grace of giving. The people stood up weeping and emptying their wallets. They were stirred in their hearts by God, and everyone gave all they possibly could as they were moved upon by the Lord. I had heard of things like this happening, but I had never before witnessed it.

In the morning when I came down to do the broadcast,[29] there were more people waiting for me. People I had never seen before, telling me that the Lord had awakened them and that they had no peace until they brought the money to me. What these people gave amounted to many thousands of dollars. When the doubting contractor arrived, his money was ready for him, as it had been for all the others. Thus we were made to know afresh that God's callings are His enabling. What He has promised to do, He is able to fulfill.

* * *

At the time the Armory was being built, obtaining steel was still a problem due to the shortages after the war years. Steel was at a premium in both cost and availability. Many times we could get only one small piece from a box load of steel. But we knew the materials for the Armory were already provided by God. To the amazement of all who were watching and predicting that it would never be built, we saw the steel come in. We saw the fabrication of it; we saw the day when it was delivered to the site.

---

[29] The "America To Your Knees" broadcast on WJLB from 10:00 a.m. to 10:30 a.m.

A Hand On My Shoulder

I shall never forget the day they brought the tremendous piece of fabricated steel that was to support the balcony. It weighed about 20 tons. We had to have the police clear a way through the streets as it was brought up. I sat in a car across the street and watched them swing the huge piece of steel by electric hoists, as men standing on precarious perches waited for the steel to swing into position where they could take hold of it and fasten it in place. I cried out to God in prayer that none should be hurt, because we had been warned that on jobs as large as this one, or more, fatality was inevitable. But God was good. When the work was completed, there was not one worker with even an injury. They all called it a miracle. With every part of the work, God gave wisdom to the workman and the finances to pay his hire. With the problems of availability of materials and craftsmanship, He also proved faithful.

* * *

When the time came for the delicate task of the acoustic plastering, we realized we were facing a tremendous problem in finding the right man to do the job. The importance of good acoustics in a building of this size and purpose was great. And of course, the cost was a major point of concern as well.

As mentioned in previous chapters, God had given us the power to deliver many helpless victims of drugs, alcohol, and nicotine. At this time, a member of another denomination on the west side of Detroit brought a man to us who had been bound by the habit of drink: he was very thin and worn. The good Christian who had brought him said, "Sister Beall, we hear that you are able to deliver men like this."

I replied, "Yes, God has been merciful every time we have prayed for such a victim."

So we prayed for this man, and he was delivered from his addiction that bound him. He was delivered, saved, and soon thereafter filled with the Holy Spirit.

Sometime later this man came to us and said he had heard we were seeking an acoustical plasterer for our building. He told us he was the kind of plasterer that we were looking for. He learned his trade in England and when actively engaged in this trade, he was considered one of the best. He took my husband to see some of his work. It was evident that, indeed, he had been one of the very best. He offered to do our building, and we knew that God had answered our prayer by delivering this man.

He did a beautiful job. Everyone who looks upon the work realizes that God surely gave this man the ability and wisdom to perform an outstandingly wonderful creation of art in this plastering. He gave us a building where the acoustics are as nearly perfect as in any building we have ever been in. And so we repeat, with a heart full of thanks and praise, that God's ways are perfect.

Chapter 26

The Answering Of Many Questions

The Revival tide was mounting as the Armory was going on to completion. The building was plastered and the floor was laid. The interior began to take the shape of a sanctuary where God would dwell. I felt definitely that the decorating and the furnishings for this Temple of God should require much of my personal time, attention, and prayer. I was very zealous that the carpeting, draperies, decorating, and the furnishings should in every detail reflect our love, esteem, and appreciation to God and to all who had so loyally given of their time, their prayers, and finances to make this Armory a memorial to His faithfulness. The time for the dedication services for the Temple was drawing near. We were all eagerly working toward that great day.

In the midst of this, I received a telephone call from an evangelist, Vera Ludlum, who was a member of the religious organization we had joined, the Assemblies of God. She said she had heard from her mother and father in Canada that God was moving there in revival power in a way that the church had never before seen. They invited her to come to witness this supernatural moving of God. During our telephone conversation, she told me they were driving to Canada, and since the back seat of their car was empty, she and her husband would like to take me with them. I was immediately stirred to tell her there would be no possibility of my going: we were at a most crucial time in our building program where I felt I was definitely needed every minute. Besides, I felt it impossible to ride in the back seat of the car as it made me very ill. I was ready to give her the reasons why I couldn't possibly go, when the Lord spoke to me:

"You go! I came that you might have life and have it more abundantly."[30] I didn't know what connection this Scripture had with the Lord urging me to go, but I knew the Lord had spoken to me.

So instead of telling her all the reasons why I couldn't go, I thanked her for the invitation and said I would be very happy to go along with her and her husband. She told me this outstanding Revival was in Vancouver, but I didn't realize when I said yes that it was Vancouver, British Columbia!

In the days that followed, I began to make arrangements for my departure. While I was gone, I needed someone to take my place in the church. I had no one to minister at the pulpit or anyone to take our radio broadcasts. (My son Jim was not in the ministry at this time.) However, I prayed, and the Lord showed me where I could get someone for both the pulpit and the radio. This presented a real problem for the person who was to take my place, but I told him that God had spoken to me and would remove all hindrances. We both realized it would have to be a miracle. But, of course, we are serving a miracle-working God. Right on time He performed the miracle that was needed to make it possible for this person to come to Detroit and to be there until I returned.

The Lord smoothed out every difficulty, and in no time I was ready to leave with my friends. I often think if I had known what was going to come from this trip to Vancouver, in blessing and in sorrow, in losing old friends and gaining new ones, I wonder what my reaction to the invitation would have been. It certainly is the blessing of an all-knowing God that we do not know what tomorrow holds, for I am sure in our human fear of suffering and misunder-standing, we would hesitate to do the thing that would ultimately bring us and so many others much blessing and help. I personally have thanked God many times that I did not know the result of that Vancouver trip before I went. I have thanked Him that I did go and that He was able by His grace to trust me with so tremendous a responsibility. The results of the Revival in Vancouver brought to the lives of many a complete change in their beliefs and their mode of worship.

* * *

---

[30] See John 10:10

A Hand On My Shoulder

The church in Vancouver was Glad Tidings Tabernacle, pastored by Rev. Hugh Layzelle. It was an Assembly of God church, as were we in Detroit. We had no thought at any time that we were doing anything contrary to the rules and regulation of the Official Headquarters of our denomination and the belief of the people with whom we were in fellowship.

When we walked into that little humble church in Vancouver, we were met by the lovely presence of God in the meetings. In fact, I had never before in my life sensed the presence and power of God as I did in that church. The worship was heavenly, the teaching so down-to-earth and so full of truth, that we certainly felt we had come into a new realm—into another one of His lovely chambers of revelation and truth. The services continued until midnight; even then it seemed hard to leave and wait until the next morning. It was an experience I shall never forget, for I met God in a new way. It answered to my heart's satisfaction many of the questions that were constantly in my mind concerning the things God had asked me to do. Many of the undertakings that I was doing in blind faith and obedience were now being revealed to me. I received an understanding of many things that had caused me to lie awake night after night. Yes, God met me!

* * *

One day I was sitting in the congregation thinking in my heart of the command God had given to build the Armory where soldiers would receive equipment. As I thought on this, there swept over me such a realization that I had really no equipment of my own. So many times I had felt the need greater than what I had in the way of helping others in deliverance and healing. While I thought on these things and expressed my need in the meeting, they called me to come forward. The Presbytery[31] laid hands on me. Among the many things that were prophesied, one part of the prophecy was almost more than I could receive. These men who had never been to Detroit, who never at any time had seen the building that God called an Armory, a building almost in a state of completion, began to prophesy about it:

---

[31] Ministers and church leaders

The Answering Of Many Questions

"They shall come to thee from the ends of the earth and shall go forth from thee as lions equipped as from a mighty Armory."[32]

My heart seemed to overflow because of the greatness of God in granting to my heart this great confirmation and encouragement. Also prophesied were the gifts of wisdom and knowledge, discernment of spirits, and healing. This prophecy regarding the gift of healing was a definite confirmation of a burning I had been feeling in my hands for some weeks, almost to the point of a burning ache. It seemed to be relieved when some were prayed for and received their healing. I still have the sign in my hands until this day and will say further that I have seen in a measure of confirmation all that was spoken and prophesied that day.

I also learned that walls do not stop the prophetic word. When it was prophesied that "they would come from the ends of the earth," certainly God's Word went forth to the ends of the world, even as it did when God spoke to Noah and told him that two by two every living thing would come to him to the Ark. I have often wondered what means of transportation Noah used to bring all of these animals over the world, every species, into the Ark, but I never understood until then that it was because God had sent out His Word and said it would be so. Animals and every living thing left their place of habitation and started for the Ark to fulfill the Word of God that had gone forth to Noah. When the Ark was ready, the animals were there ready to enter the Ark, and then God shut the door.

So it was with the Armory. When I returned from the meetings in Vancouver, people began to come from the ends of the earth to the Armory to have hands laid on them and the prophetic Word to go over them. They came to receive an impartation of spiritual

---

[32] Hugh Layzell confirms Myrtle's account in his book *Sons of His Purpose*. He states, "After a day or two, the brethren agreed to minister to her in presbytery. Audrey and I remember this incident very well. As soon as she knelt before the presbyters, Ern Hawtin began to prophesy. He said, (something like this) 'Has not the Lord called you to build for Him an armory, where His last day army will be trained and equipped with the gifts of the Spirit in order to take the gospel to the ends of the earth in these last days?' This was, in effect, the very word she had received from the Lord concerning the Church in Detroit."
Sons of Purpose by Hugh and Audrey Layzell, CreateSpace Independent Publishing Platform, June 8, 2013, Chapter 11.

equipment, to be given them in words of confirmation by the Spirit through the words of the Presbytery. They continued to come and fill the auditorium from morning to night.

For three-and-a-half years they came! We did not know who they were or where they came from until they would make it known in the meeting just who they were, what part of the country they were from, and just why and how they got there. We were made conscious of the fact that it was the Word of God that had gone forth and impressed their hearts to come to Detroit—to come to God's spiritual Armory where they would get equipment for the "warfare" that lay ahead for the Sons of God. They waited before the Lord from morning until night with fasting. Even District Presbyters (pastors, directors) came with their whole Presbytery (church leaders) from different states. The testimony of all was: they met God as they entered the doors. This was a great hour of restoration of the power and gifts of the Holy Spirit in His Church.

* * *

Note: At the first service after mother's return from Vancouver, December 5, 1948, we gathered together in the Basement Church with great expectancy, eager to hear what had happened in Vancouver. My brother Jim opened the service and asked the people to stand. Suddenly everyone in the building started singing praises to God. This spiritual worship and praise, which was unheard of at this time, continued for about an hour. Then Mrs. Tubby went to the piano and was inspired to sing:

> *This is the promise of the coming Latter Rain,*
> *Lift up your eyes, behold the ripening grain,*
> *Many signs and wonders in His mighty Name,*
> *Drink, oh drink, my people, for this is Latter Rain.*

In her message that momentous morning, Mother shared her experience in Vancouver. She told how moved she had been by the presence of God and the fresh revelation of teaching. But, most of all, with great excitement she gave testimony of how the Word she had been given by God to "build an armory" was confirmed through prophecy spoken by men who knew nothing of the project. Although there had been a revival that began years earlier at Bethesda, this Sunday marked the beginning of what would be known as a Latter Rain Revival

—a revival marked by a new sound of worship, the laying on of hands with prophecy, and a restoration of the gifts of the Holy Spirit. (Patricia Beall Gruits)

Chapter 27

Dedication Of The Temple

We were blessed with a tremendous revival, totally unexpected and unplanned just as our Temple, the Armory, was nearing completion. At first we feared that the Revival might hinder our efforts toward the rapid fulfillment of our long-awaited dream. Even before the Revival, it had seemed as though there were not enough minutes in a day: so many tasks remained to be performed, so many details cried for our attention. It seemed we could not possibly assume another undertaking. Yet, as both the Revival and the work on the Temple progressed, we seemed to draw strength from the one to complete the other. The two projects seemed to parallel each other, forming a track as it were, to guide our daily efforts.

With God's benevolence and guidance, we were able to supervise the interior decoration of the Temple, yet give our undivided attention to the meetings which were being held day and night. True, there were times when it seemed that weariness would force me to slacken my pace, to neglect something. Then it seemed as though I would receive a refreshing from some supernatural well, and once again I would have the strength to drive forward. Again and again I saw it proved that "His callings are His enabling." Finally, the end was in sight. With a joy that defies all description, we announced that the opening service would be held on the afternoon of Sunday, February 13, 1949.

No sooner had we set a date for the opening than time seemed to rush by even more quickly than before. On the day before the scheduled opening much still remained to be done, so much that I feared it could not be accomplished in time. There were drapes to be hung; there were still seats to be washed; and there were so many

Dedication Of The Temple

other time-consuming tasks too numerous to mention. The more we thought about the work still lay ahead of us, the more we despaired that we would be able to finish it in time for the opening for which so many people had waited so long.

From time to time, I pictured myself as a tightrope walker performing on a high wire. At one end of my balancing pole was the Revival, at the other was the Temple, equally demanding of my time and strength. Far below, my congregation urged me on, while I prayed to God to guide every footstep in this tremendous undertaking. But now the picture was being completed, and the end was only a step away. Slowly I gazed around the building: first at the majestic new organ just waiting for the first thundering chord to be struck, next at the splendid new piano, then at the handsome pulpit from where I hoped to speak the Word of God. My eyes swept across the new carpeting, a $5,000 expenditure. Then up along the magnificent draperies which cost an equal amount.

Finally my eyes came to rest upon the beautiful hand painting of where Christ was baptized at the Jordan, now in its place of honor upon the wall. It did not seem possible that all of this splendor, all of this comfort and beauty could belong to us—a group who had experienced the humblest of beginnings in the smallest, most barren of churches, where there had not even been songbooks, let alone an organ or piano. Still even harder to recall, there had not even been chairs to sit on or a pulpit to speak from. Our only credit had been our clean floors, kept immaculate by frequent and vigorous scrubbings. But right here I want to say how God was just as much among us there in our humble surroundings as He would be in this beautiful building.

With renewed zeal, we plunged in to help with the work that remained to be done. All through the day we worked, pausing only for a hastily prepared lunch. Through Saturday night and well into Sunday morning we worked, attending to every last minor detail. Then finally all was in readiness. Exhausted but exultant, we stood back to take one last look at what had taken so much hard work and so long to accomplish. Once again I gazed unbelievingly at this dream that had now become a reality. How I wished that our organist were there to strike up a triumphant march! Then I realized that my real joy was not in knowing that we had built a beautiful Temple, but in knowing that we were serving God, in knowing that He was with us now just as He had been with us in the little church so many years ago. There can be no joy in any accomplishment or in any possessions unless we have God's presence.

Even though we were fatigued from our long hours of work, we were reluctant to leave the Temple and take what little rest our excited minds would permit us. When I awoke Sunday morning, however, there was no question of fatigue, but rather a feeling of apprehension and expectation. In my mind I was asking myself over and over again, "Where will we get enough people to fill a place as large as this?"

When I arrived at the Temple, this fear stayed with me. Rather than see for myself, I walked up to a young lady who was seated at the piano and asked, "Are there many here yet?"

She turned to me very nonchalantly and said, "It's full."

My ears did not believe her. I thought perhaps she had misunderstood me. So I said, "You do not understand what I just asked. Are there many people in the auditorium yet?"

Again she replied, "It's full!"

I was still convinced she had not understood my question, so I decided to try another approach and asked, "How about the balcony? Is there anyone up there yet?"

Once again she turned around to face me, this time rather impatiently. Then very slowly and deliberately, she stated, "I said, it's FULL!"

And full it was! To my utter amazement, we walked out on the platform to find that every available seat in the main auditorium had been taken and extra chairs had been set up in the aisles. The platform was jammed. The balcony was filled. People were sitting on the stairway to the balcony and lined up against the back wall, even the foyer was full. The downstairs auditorium[33] was filled to capacity. These people were reached by a loudspeaker. Even more impressive, the bus drivers from the DSR (Detroit's City trans-portation system) turned away 1,700 people by actual ticker count.

When my senses had stopped swirling, I heard the murmur of the thousands assembled before me. They were marveling in whispers at the splendor and the presence of God that surrounded them. My

---

[33] The "downstairs auditorium" refers to the main auditorium of the Basement Church.

Dedication Of The Temple

own happiness and gratitude soared until it seemed it could no longer be contained. As the second hand raced one last time around the clock, I rejoiced inwardly with our Father that we had been able to carry out His instructions. The Armory was open!

* * *

The day of dedication of the Temple will be a day never to be forgotten by all who were able to get into the buildings, and even by those who were not able to get in. They saw the Hand of God in causing this enormous Armory to be erected. They saw God stir the hearts of people everywhere, to fill not only the new Temple but also the lower auditorium. They saw the multitude still longing to get in, but turned away because there was no room.

Not only was the Temple filled to capacity with people, but it was also filled with the glory and presence of God. Such singing, such worshiping of God, such prophecies, such supernatural utterances as we heard from the lips of God's ordained ministers will always remain the greatest wonderment of our lives. It seemed the time just flew. People were being saved, filled with the Holy Spirit, confirmed, and delivered. Everyone was ministering to one another. God let us see by actual demonstration before our very eyes the ministry of the Body of Christ. The teaching of the Body of Christ[34] had not been much in evidence up until this time, but God began to teach through His ministers, by precept and example, the tremendous truths of the hour. Never had we heard such preaching.

The building was jammed at every service throughout the day. It just seemed the day was too short. Far into the night people could be found here and there in the building waiting before God, wanting their portion. Certainly this was a day of heaven on earth. We called the building "A Memorial to His Faithfulness," and everyone present

---

[34] The teaching of the Body of Christ is that Jesus is the Head of the Church and His Church is made up of different "parts." Some people are called to be apostles, prophets, evangelists, pastors, or teachers for the purpose of perfecting (maturing) believers. Others are called to the ministry of helps, government (administration), healing, mercy, etc. Though our gifts may be different, though our callings are not the same, we are to operate in unity, to function as one.

A Hand On My Shoulder

with one consent said, "Yes, we have seen the faithfulness of God as never before."

In the weeks that followed, we had to have police protection and help to empty the building for ventilation between services and to give those who had not been able to attend one service the opportunity of getting into the next service. We had services day and night. Never in my life have I seen people so full of expectancy, so hungry, so anxious to hear from God, as we saw in these early days of this Latter Rain Revival.

God was doing a new thing in the earth. We saw denominational barriers and color barriers fade into oblivion as God poured out His Spirit. We saw the Body of Jesus Christ as we never saw it before. We saw that in Christ there is no division. There is neither male nor female, bond nor free, Jew nor Greek. We saw that by the Spirit of God we are indeed made One! We saw the division because of doctrine, methods, and traditions fade away as each one of us was made conscious of Whom and in Whom we believe. We found that in getting our faith centered where it should be centered, our faith put back in God where it should be, the other things about which we did not agree seemed very trivial and of less importance.

We saw groups who had been baptized under different formulas coming together with an understanding that we had all been baptized by faith into the Lord Jesus Christ. People whom we could neither love nor fellowship with, we suddenly found to be our brothers and sisters in the Lord. We saw for the first time that division is an awful thing. We found the denominational barriers gone, and we realized that we belonged to the Church of the Lord Jesus Christ. We were beginning to understand, by what we were seeing demonstrated and by what we were hearing preached, the reason God asked us to build an Armory to seat so many—a place where "soldiers of the Cross" would get their spiritual equipment. It seemed this same understanding came to the multitude of people who attended our Dedication Convention which began on that glorious Sunday, February 13, 1949.

Note: The actual seating in the sanctuary turned out to be less than 3,000 people --much to Myrtle's dismay. When Bethesda moved from Detroit to Sterling Heights in 1989, an essential requirement of the building program was for the sanctuary to seat 3,000 people to fulfill the number God had given Myrtle so long ago.

Dedication Of The Temple

Bethesda Missionary Temple – View from Van Dyke Avenue

Bethesda Missionary Temple – View from Nevada Avenue

Chapter 28

Miracles And Multitudes

Many miracles were performed during the Convention which occupied several months following the Dedication Day of the Temple on February 13, 1949. It was a time of supernatural confirmations of faith too numerous to mention. God was stirring our hearts to believe, and He was getting the glory.

One such occurrence concerned a young lad who was brought to the Convention from Canada by his father. During his visit to the Temple, hands were laid upon him for release and healing. His father took him home in faith. This boy had been born with one limb shorter than the other by a few inches. There was no earthly cure for his condition. But on the morning of the day following the laying on of hands for healing, the boy came downstairs from his bedroom. To the utter amazement of his family, they found that God had performed a miracle in the night. Both his legs were now the same length!

This was a wonderful miracle of healing—a complete and prompt correction by God of a physical condition that the doctors apparently had given up as hopeless. The family of the boy was so transported by the goodness of God that they sent us the testimony, and the case received widespread publicity. Even one of the leading news commentators of one of the large radio stations in Detroit gave forth the story of this miracle as one of the top news items of the day.

A District Superintendent of the Wisconsin Assemblies of God came to the Temple, along with his Presbytery, to investigate and observe firsthand what he had heard to be a great move of God. His testimony was terse, straightforward, and spoken without a doubt or hesitation. "I ran into God!" he declared, and then added, "I'd hate

Miracles And Multitudes

to think I didn't know God when I met Him!" This man went back to Wisconsin with his Presbytery on fire for God, determined to do God's will and to identify himself with that which God was doing in the earth. Many new churches were opened up all over the world following the Convention where the great truth of the Ministry of the Body of Jesus Christ with all the gifts of the Spirit were taught and demonstrated.

* * *

During this time, when the overflow crowds were so mighty because so many were being saved and healed, we had to move the Sunday meeting to the Coliseum at the State Fair Grounds in Detroit, where there was seating for 10,000. Yet even this tremendous capacity was not enough to accommodate the crowds. Every available seat was taken in the balconies and in the main auditorium. Thousands stood along the walls as well. Never before had we seen such a demonstration of the moving of the Spirit of God over the people. At the close of this epoch-making meeting, when the people were asked who among them would like to make a decision for Christ, they left their seats or their positions by the walls, and came down the aisles in droves. I never saw the like of this demonstration in my life—no, not ever!

They filled the inquiry rooms.[35] When one was occupied to capacity, they would be directed to another inquiry room clear across the great auditorium. Without confusion, but with great determination and calmness, not one broke ranks, but all marched from one inquiry room to another until they had filled the rooms on the north, east, west, and south sides of the auditorium. When every inch of available space where people could be prayed with had been taken, one group of very well-dressed women who could find no place in any of the inquiry rooms said to a worker who was standing by, "Is there no place for us? Is there no one who cares for our souls?"

They were standing near a hamburger stand where the remains of sandwiches, hot dogs, and waste paper had been thrown on the floor and under the counter. The worker looked around, and seeing no

---

[35] Inquiry rooms were allocated areas in the Coliseum where people could be prayed for individually.

available space but a littered hamburger stand, answered the women, "Well, there doesn't seem to be any space but this!" Then and there, even in such unbecoming surroundings, these well-dressed women knelt among the debris beneath the counter of a hamburger stand and gave their hearts to the Lord.

Such scenes were repeated throughout the Coliseum. By the end of the meeting there were some two thousand who had prayed through to an actual experience. So the Revival continued to mount without diminishing, reaching proportions we never thought possible to witness in our day. God was doing the "exceeding abundantly" beyond all that we could expect or wish. In the days that followed, people came from everywhere to receive the confirmation of their call and ministry. Gifts of the Spirit were received by the laying on of hands and by prophecy, arming believers with spiritual strength and power. They left the Convention with a new determination, a new zeal, and a new vision, having seen God in reality.

Without publishing any advertisements, sending out invitations or dispersing handbills, without any publicity except that which was inspired by the personal experiences of our visitors repeated by word of mouth, and by the news releases of radio commentators, newspaper reporters, and similar agencies, we found people flocking to our doors from every part of the world. Over and over again we saw the fulfillment of that prophecy given to us in Vancouver: "They shall come to thee from the ends of the earth and will go out from thee as lions equipped as from a mighty armory."

Truly Bethesda Missionary Temple had become an Armory.

Chapter 29

He is the Same Yesterday, Today, and Forever

It seems to be a human characteristic that few of us are capable of steadily sustained effort toward a goal. We move in impulses like alternating electric current: sometimes these impulses are close together, sometimes spread over a wider period. We receive sudden inspiration, a fresh drive, and we accomplish a great deal in a short time. Then there comes a static period until the next impulse comes, when we advance slowly if at all.

Not everyone, but most of us, climbs to God in a series of stages, actuated by some special grace or revelation that inspires us to vigorously mount to the next height. For example, we may be instrumental in saving a difficult soul, a new road may be suddenly revealed to us, a different insight may clarify a question troubling us, a signal of God's omniscience and omnipotence may be demonstrated to us in some dramatic way. Then with joy and great encouragement in His goodness and power, we leap ahead with enthusiasm and new energy to do His service.

In this regard I have often said that there is nothing in the world that gives a person a new impetus in carrying on God's work than the miracle of a divine healing or deliverance. However, our tendency is to think of God's miracles as events more or less related to olden times, ancient history occurring in the pages of the Old and New Testaments when saints and prophets walked the earth, and God was very close to man. The old Biblical faith, trust, and hope in God as our only refuge and relief from cataclysms of nature, the ravages of mysterious diseases, and the tragic consequences of an accident have been transferred by many to the achievements of science, medicine, and invention. The "miracles" accomplished by these lofty pursuits of man in the nineteenth and twentieth centuries are not to be denied, nor their results in the increased health, happiness, and safety of today's common man.

But all of us are aware that there are times when all of man's worldly knowledge becomes bewildered and powerless, and we turn to God as our final desperate hope. In the old days man turned to God more frequently, believing in and appealing to Him in every suffering, frustration, and disappointment. Today, with our habit of seeking human help in many of our daily difficulties, we do not go so often to God, and we wonder sometimes if perhaps God, too, has gotten out of the habit of miracles.

As I have put pen and paper retracing my journey with the Lord, I can state with full conviction that God is not out of the habit of miracles. Throughout my life and ministry, God has proven His faithfulness by performing miracles of provision, deliverance, and divine healing. To underscore this conviction, I want to share yet two more instances of God's miracle-working power in my life.

* * *

Shortly after I was saved and about two months before our last child was born, I endeavored to climb up a chair, when the rung broke beneath my feet, and its jagged end pierced my limb, causing a deep, nasty wound that later developed into a running ulcer. After repeated visits to the doctor, after many treatments in an effort to relieve and cure the condition without any success, the doctor reluctantly informed me that I had an ulcer which would probably give me trouble the rest of my life.

On each visit he would clean out the wound, treat and dress it, and make it comfortable under an elastic stocking. He said this was all that could be done for me. Then he invariably followed this with a warning of what an awful thing I could expect for the rest of my life because of this unfortunate accident. This man was a scientist, and his conclusions were based on up-to-date medical knowledge. He desire was not to frighten or depress me but merely prepare my mind for a condition I would have to put up with in the future. Some years before, I would have believed him without question and accepted the fact that I would have to live with this painful and troublesome thing for all the years to come.

But at this time I had just found Jesus Christ as my Savior and Baptizer. I was told that He was also a Healer, just as He was when He was upon the earth. I believed, and I was prayed for by one of God's servants and assured that God had heard our prayers. By the time I was due to make the next visit to the doctor, it appeared to me certainly as though God had definitely heard us and that the healing was surely taking place.

In the modern, scientific atmosphere of the doctor's office, while waiting to be called, it was difficult to maintain the spiritual conviction which I had had before I left my home for this visit. Surely I thought, this place is one the shrines of modern medicine, and this man's knowledge, training, experience, and research qualifies him more than I to decide whether this condition was capable of healing. But then I reflected that his point of view did not take into consideration the spiritual fact of a miracle; it was based on worldly logic and reasoning only. Besides, had I not seen the evidence with my own eyes in the changed appearance of the wound? So when I entered his private office, as he was making ready to dress the limb as usual, I said to him, "Doctor, I believe that my limb is healed."

He laughed and said kindly, "There is no use in doing any wishful thinking about this. You have something here for the rest of your life."

Then he opened up the bandages and looked at the wound. His eyes opened wide in amazement and with a low whistle he remarked incredulously, "Why, this is certainly a healing scab."

And then, in a half-embarrassed effort to laugh it off, he said, "That sure is some Vaseline that I have been using on this limb."

I said to him, "Doctor, do you honestly believe it was the Vaseline that has accomplished this remarkable cure?"

He answered with a sober frankness, "No, but I wouldn't know what else to credit it to."

Then I told him how I had found the Lord Jesus Christ to be the same today as He was when He would heal all who came to Him. I related how I had been prayed for by one of the servants of God and had noticed a definite improvement in my condition after a lack of success by his medical efforts.

He was very impressed and said, "Well, more power to you."

A Hand On My Shoulder

During one particular winter season I was suffering with sinus trouble. The pain and distress were indescribable. There seemed to be no respite or relief for me, no matter what I did. Those who have gone through this type of illness will understand what I mean when I say that attack followed attack with the excruciating pain. I had been prayed for and was reluctant to ask for medical help, because I believed I would be delivered of my misery through divine intervention. However, because of the continuous, unbearable pain, it seemed I was forced to be willing to appeal for medical help. I finally consented to visit a sinus specialist, because I feared I might lose my mind due to the terrific pain.

The doctor examined me thoroughly and discovered I had a blocked nasal atrium. The secretions discharged by the infected area had hardened in the channel between my nose and ear. As past sinus sufferers are unhappily aware, this location is very difficult to access for treatment. The specialist tried the lights and everything else he knew for external treatment until it seemed that my eyeball was being forced out of the socket. In fact, so terrible was the pressure and so sure was I that my eye was actually protruding, I would look in the mirror for verification that the eye was in its proper position.

After this initial visit to the doctor, I returned home and remained in bed until what little relief he had been able to give me wore off. Then I would struggle out of bed and return for another treatment. This routine went on for some time until it became evident to both the doctor and myself that it was of no use. Finally he confessed that the treatment was not accomplishing any lasting good and the cause of the trouble was not being reached. On this occasion he informed me that the only thing left to do was to operate the following morning.

Before I left his office, he gave me some pills and instructed me to take them just before I left the house the next morning and to eat no breakfast in preparation for the operation. I told him I could not promise to appear for the operation. He could not understand my reluctance to be operated on, but I had not yet given up faith that God would Himself intervene. However, I did assure the doctor that I would telephone him first thing in the morning and advise him of my decision.

I returned home and was helped back into bed, simply beside myself with pain and worry. I was in company of many young Chris-

He Is The Same Yesterday, Today, And Forever

tians who could not understand why there had not been an answer to the prayers which had been poured out on my behalf. I have since learned that God's delays are not denials!

That afternoon Sister Metler came to visit and pray for me. When she saw the agony I was going through, both physical and spiritual, she knelt down by my bed. I have never seen nor heard since then anything to compare with the compassion with which she appealed to the Lord for me. She sobbed out of the compassion of her heart before God, and no one could have asked for a more devoted, sincere, and passionate advocate. Before she left we both knew beyond question, with a witness in our hearts, that the Lord had heard her prayer.

Finally the time came when she had to leave, and my husband offered to drive her home. I lay there in bed, still suffering and with mixed emotions. I was convinced that God had undoubtedly heard the moving appeal which Sister Metler had poured out for me, and yet the pain had not subsided. Every passing moment brought me closer to the time when I would have to admit defeat and submit to the operation. After a time I had another visitor, a friend who was a practical nurse. As she came into the room and sat down beside my bed, she looked at me curiously and asked why I was using so much Kleenex. I replied that it seemed necessary. Then I realized it had only been in the past little while since Sister Metler had left that my consumption of the paper tissues had grown so profuse.

My visitor looked at me closely. Then her face brightened and she declared, "Well, praise God. It's opened!" And indeed it had. The obstruction had begun to dissolve and discharge itself normally. God had performed a miracle! The pain began to ease gradually, and in an amazingly short time I was completely without pain.

* * *

When Jesus Christ walked this earth, he performed great miracles of forgiveness, deliverance, and healing. And He still has the power and inclination to do the same today. Over and over again, throughout my life, God had proved to me, my friends, and loved ones that He is "the same yesterday, today, and forever." *(Heb. 13:8)* He isn't just a God of the past; He is the God of our present.

Chapter 30

Reminisces: Thanksgiving 1956

On the eve of this Thanksgiving in the year of our Lord 1956, I feel that today is a great vantage point from which one may view the tremendous panorama of God's goodness—past, present, and future. What lies ahead in the beneficence of God can be measured only by that which has been bestowed on us in the past. Should the future hold blessings comparable to that which have gone before, I am sure that our thankfulness to the Lord will know no bounds.

We count our blessings, it seems to me, far too seldom. Once a year is not nearly enough to review the gifts and graces the Lord in His love has seen fit to bestow upon us. Still, at Thanksgiving time it seems a particularly appropriate moment to do so and to render our grateful appreciation for His blessings. And so as I sit here reminiscing over the past, the many marks of God's favor crowd in upon me. My heart is filled to overflowing with awe and gratitude. Though the way has sometimes been difficult and puzzling, I can look back and see that each time an insurmountable obstacle appeared in the path, God's *Hand* was promptly extended to raise me over it.

I see the pattern of my life, from earliest childhood, being woven together by incidents which at that time seemed a little strange, and yet one seemed powerless to take any other road. Even as a child, the *Hand* on my shoulder guided me firmly and unerringly away from the lanes of aimlessness and the bypaths of frustration, and led me back upon the highway of God's main route.

But in remembering this and the countless other blessings, large and small, which the Lord in His love has visited upon me during my lifetime, I am thinking especially today of the great goodness which He showed in surrounding me with a family who have been a great source of satisfaction and affection through a trying and sometimes wearing journey.

I remember the day on which my eldest child, Patricia Doris, was saved and the time she was baptized in the Holy Spirit. God kindly allowed me to be with her when He was filling her with the Spirit; and I saw through its manifestation the very carefulness of God as He granted her, a young girl, the strong power to be His witness. I have watched her since as she has grown with Him and observed her choices along the way that were well directed by God in advance of her decisions. I saw her enter into a God-ordained ministry of writing Sunday School literature, the Latter Rain Evangel, and the PeterPat series of children's books, as well as all the educational material for the Confirmation classes. Likewise, I have seen her ministry and burden for the youth grow, and now as a young mother, she is directing her four sons to also walk in the Way.

FOR THIS, LORD, I AM GRATEFUL!

Then I reflect upon my eldest son, James Lee. He was a weak, sickly child, and we despaired many times that we would never succeed in raising him to manhood. Today I recall our great thankfulness in seeing the faithfulness of God in bringing him out of all this weakness into the strength of a good man.

I recall also the night James Lee failed to return home on time from the Young People's Meeting at the church. I was much worried and concerned at the thought of what may have befallen him and prayed earnestly to God for his protection. At midnight he came home and dashed up the stairs to me, taking two or three steps at a time; he was crying, "Mother, I've got Him. Mother, I've got Him!" I met Jim at the top of the staircase. Suddenly his arms were around me as he sobbed, "Mother, God has given me the precious Holy Spirit and has called me to help you in the work!"

God had indeed given him a vision that night of the burden that the Lord had put upon me. Jim had cried out to God that he might help me carry this burden. Right then and there the Lord baptized him in the Holy Spirit.

A few years later, just as he was about to graduate from high school, Jim prepared to enter the Navy in World War II. It was a terribly bitter experience for me, and I felt it was more than I could stand. Then God whispered to me: "I will keep what you commit to me against that day."³⁶ He anointed me to make the committal, and the peace of God entered my heart. I knew without further doubt that Jim was safe in God's hands and would come back.

I see him later, having returned—restless, confused, and seeking his niche in life. Then God spoke to Jim again, calling him to the ministry, and he accepted the call.

FOR THIS LORD, I AM GRATEFUL!

Then my thoughts turn to our youngest child, our son Harry, who was called by God when a mere boy. Harry was baptized in the Holy Spirit as a young boy, receiving with the Baptism a burden to help others to receive the Holy Spirit. The Lord has given him a ministry of song and the teaching and preaching of the Word.

I remember as I sit here the day when his final decision was made. He had attended Bible College in Waxahachie, Texas and had returned still restless, still unsettled as to his future. On this day he decided to enroll in Wayne University to study to be a high school teacher. After enrolling, he returned home and told me what he had done. Looking into his face, I knew his decision had not answered the question in his heart. As I saw him sitting there with the burden of his decision heavy upon him, and yet without the satisfaction of having done what he really wished, my heart ached for him.

So I asked Harry, "Son, would you like Mother to pray with you?" He answered that he would. We went upstairs to my study, fell upon our knees in prayer, and God met us. Harry said "yes" to God and farewell to the college, and entered into God's ministry.

FOR THIS, LORD, I AM GRATEFUL!

It blesses me to remember the faithfulness of God in choosing a Christian mate for each one of my children and to see their children raised for God.

FOR THIS, LORD, I AM GRATEFUL!

---

³⁶ See 2 Timothy 1:12

Finally, as I sit here reminiscing over the past, I remember how God caused me to choose the mate He had ordained for me, Harry Beall. It was a strange way in which God accomplished this purpose, but His Word says, "Ye have not chosen me, but I have chosen you, and ordained you, that ye go and bring forth much fruit. . . " *(John 15:16)*

As I think of my husband and the goodness of God that was shown to him—how the Lord called him, raised him from his deathbed, and laid upon his heart the burden of the engineering and construction of the great spiritual plant here in Detroit.

FOR THIS, LORD, I AM GRATEFUL!

Myrtle Dorthea Monville Beall

* * *

Throughout the Scriptures God instructs us to remember what He has done. How blessed we are to have this account to remember God's faithfulness to a woman who felt God's Hand on her life and responded to it.

How blessed we are that the God who touched her life continues to touch our lives today.

FOR THIS, LORD, I AM GRATEFUL!

K. Joy Hughes Gruits

Harry and Pastor M.D. Beall

Pastor M.D. Beall

Harry and Myrtle Beall

CHRONOLOGY

December 9, 1894   Myrtle Dorthea Monville is born in Hubbell, Michigan.

June 1910   Myrtle graduates at the age of 16 from Lake Linden High School.

June 15, 1920   Myrtle Monville marries Harry Lee Beall at the Episcopal Methodist Church.

June 14, 1934   Bethesda (Missionary) Tabernacle opens. The original storefront church would later be referred to as the Mission Building.

1936   The Portable Church is bought and moved.

1937   An addition is built onto the Portable Church.

1939   The Basement Church is built.

1948   Construction of the Armory; the Sanctuary of Bethesda Missionary Temple.

November 1948   M.D. Beall (Myrtle) travels to Vancouver, B.C.

December 1948   In the Basement Church a Latter Rain Revival begins.

February 13, 1949   Dedication of the Armory, the Sanctuary of Bethesda Missionary Temple. Latter Rain Revival services continue day and night for the next 3 ½ years.

1949-1950	Bethesda becomes an independent church, ending its affiliation with the Assemblies of God.
1951	First issue of the *Latter Rain Evangel* is published by Evangel Press established by Peter and Patricia Beall Gruits.
1952	The first gymnasium, the Recreation Center, is built.
1955	Patricia Beall Gruits teaches the first Youth Catechism class with material that would be developed into the book, *Understanding God*.
June 1958	Bethesda is pictured in an article in the national magazine, LIFE (the June 9th edition). The article was titled: "The Third Force in Christendom."
1959	Patricia Beall Gruits teaches the first Adult Catechism Class.
1962	Lightning strikes and sets the Basement Building (Church) on fire. It turned out to be a blessing, making possible a four-story Education Building to be erected in its place.
1962	The 1st edition of *Understanding God* is published.
1964	The Education Building is completed.
September 1979	M.D. Beall, Myrtle Dorthea (Monville) Beall, passes away after 45 years of faithful pastoring of Bethesda Missionary Temple.
1979	M.D. Beall is written about in the book *A Walk Across America* by Peter Jenkins.

1989   The sanctuary of Bethesda Christian Church in Sterling Heights, Michigan, formally known as Bethesda Missionary Temple, is dedicated, fulfilling the word given to M.D. Beall to build a sanctuary to seat 3,000.

Made in the USA
Monee, IL
22 December 2024